Praise for
"Being Single: A State For The Fragile Heart"

Being Single: A State For The Fragile Heart, A Guide to Self-love, Finding You and Purposeful Living is relevant to those seeking their own well-being and happiness, owning their truth, ending toxic relationships, letting go of painful pasts and moving on. The book is a push for us to step outside our comfort zone and embrace the flaws that make us stand out and be different. I recommend it as an insightful read for both men and women. It serves as a guide to a healthier and purposeful lifestyle.

—Paul Carrick Brunson

Being Single: A State For The Fragile Heart, A Guide to Self-love, Finding You and Purposeful Living is a must read! It will help you confront things that you have ignored for so long. Kemi shares a blueprint that will teach you how to find yourself, experience self-love and live purposefully.

—Jerone Davison,
Former NFL Player, Oakland Raiders

BEING SINGLE

A State for the Fragile Heart

A Guide to Self-Love, Finding You and Purposeful Living

KEMI SOGUNLE

Published by Kemi Sogunle

First printing, August 2015

Copyright ©2015 Kemi Sogunle

All rights reserved. No part of this book may be reproduced, scanned or distributed in any printed or electronic form without permission. Please do not participate in or encourage piracy of copyrighted materials in violation of the author's rights. Purchase only authorized editions.

LIBRARY OF CONGRESS CATALOGING-IN-PUBLICATION DATA has been applied for.

ISBN: 978-0-9909721-2-9 (Print)
ISBN: 978-0-9909721-3-6 (eBook)

Real names and identity of characters mentioned have been changed to protect their privacy.

Cover page photo credit: www.cmediausa.com
Cover design: Jeanine Henning
Formatting: Maureen Cutajar

Dedication

This book is dedicated to my love, my life and my miracle, Tobi. Giving birth to you has been one of the best things (if not the best) I have done in my life. Thank you for always speaking life to me when I need it most. I pray you read this book and let it all sink in so that you find the wisdom to live a purposeful life, just as I continue to drop the nuggets of wisdom in you daily. You are indeed a shoulder to lean on. Thank you for making me the best mom ever. I love you always.

Acknowledgements

I could not have written this book without the grace and love of God that keeps me going on a daily basis. I give Him all the glory for keeping me alive to this very day. Without Him, I am nothing, nothing at all. I have learned to tune in to hear Him speak to me more than ever before.

To my late friend, Ademola Fasina-Thomas, and his family, thank you for letting use my life-coaching skills to support you during your difficult days. To his wife, Rita Fasina-Thomas, I gained a sister whose love will never grow weary but together we will build a bond of sisterhood in His love.

To everyone I have met through life's journey that continue to encourage me, thank you. To everyone reading this book, I pray that your life will be transformed and that you will come to embrace the truth, knowing that the life you deserve already exists but you have to connect with it and truly live.

To all those who taught me directly or indirectly what life is all about and contributed to my journey so far in whatever way or shape, I say a big thank you. It all led me to who I am today and helped me connect with the real me God created while living in purpose. I am grateful.

To my family, I thank you for letting me realize during my most difficult times that it is not family that I need, but God. Connecting to God, not man, led me to my purpose and gave me the opportunity to learn to love myself irrespective of what life brings. That is what life is all about: Purpose.

Contents

INTRODUCTION		1
NUGGET 1	The Very Beginning	5
NUGGET 2	Before God Formed You	17
NUGGET 3	The Journey Begins	31
NUGGET 4	Understanding the Characters	43
NUGGET 5	Who Am I?	53
NUGGET 6	The Healing Process	73
NUGGET 7	Self-Love	83
NUGGET 8	My Journey So Far	99
NUGGET 9	What to Expect Going Forward	113
NUGGET 10	Embracing Your Singleness	131
NUGGET 11	Walking in Your Purpose	149
NUGGET 12	Building into Your Relationship	153
NUGGET 13	Bottom Line/Conclusion	159
Q & A		167
ABOUT THE AUTHOR		173

 INTRODUCTION

Have you ever felt rejected, carried a pain from your past, had your heart broken? We all have had to face a form of pain from either our childhood, a relationship we thought would last, a parent who died at an early stage of life or someone who was always there for us.

Having the fear of rejection or dealing with rejection itself can be challenging. Experiencing a painful childhood, a broken heart, or losing a parent or loved one may lead us to seek for answers and love.

You may end up seeking love in others and settling for less than you're worth. You may be looking for acceptance and affection to unburden your heart of the pain you are carrying. It is about seeking for answers, and it becomes obvious when we're teenagers that there is a need, a longing, a yearning, a desire to find a way out of the pain, yet it appears that you are locked up in a world you do not understand. You have friends you cannot really talk to about this, and finally, you find a boy or girl interested in you. This person seems to care about you more than you have ever felt before. You start to put your trust in them and it may lead to you dating, feeling like this will help to ease the pain. It may lead to sex (even though the other person may not necessarily care for you) and it serves as a listening ear, which is better than not having one.

Some of those you meet may not really care about values or self-worth, not to mention self-love. Sex seems to sell more than having real relationships. There are friend-zoning, "situationships," "sexationships," and friends with benefits, to mention a few. You actually have more options to choose from depending on what type of situation you are looking to get yourself in. However, there are those who still prefer traditional dating.

Back in the day, relationships usually started right from high school or in the same neighborhood and some of our parents ended up marrying each other. They knew from high school that they would be spending the rest of their lives together. Nowadays, very few people hold on to that tradition/value. This is because there is no solid foundation set to help the individual understand what relationships are all about, let alone love. It can be mind-boggling at times to see that the value of being in good relationships can be hard to find. Everything seems to be for convenience these days, or should I call it casual dating? (This is not really dating.) If only the foundations were laid with talks that would help, you would understand as a teenager what relationships are about or what love really means.

You may have read romantic novels, but those may no longer be applicable in the present world. There is also reality TV, which may lead you to believe in fantasizing. Someone may have hurt you in the past and now you might think everyone you meet is controlling, abusive or manipulative.

You may have created that long list and decided to stick to it without the willingness to change your mindset and let go, freeing yourself from all that you have been taught and know.

(Note: Not everyone will experience this, but I encourage everyone to take a seat and read on. You may someday share this with your children to help them understand why being single is a state for the fragile heart.)

 NUGGET 1

The Very Beginning...

For me, growing up was quite interesting. I remember my mom and my aunt (her sister) teaching us about what it was hanging around boys after we the girls started having our menstrual cycle. The talks made you cringe at the sight of a boy hanging around you. It was more of a scary feeling to want to hug a boy at that time. I later on started hanging out with my brothers and realized that there was so much more to learn from being around them.

Having attended an all-girls school also helped me learn things, especially from the older girls in the class. Some of them already had boyfriends, so it was easy to sit down and eavesdrop on their conversations. Some of them shared their escapades amongst each other and I just listened. I often wondered how they managed to do all that and still attend classes at the same time.

The Naïve You

Whether boys or girls, most of us are naïve in high school. For many, it is a time of exploration. Puberty has kicked in; the girls are becoming emotional due to hormonal changes, and are attracted to the boys they pretend to drive away. Both boys and girls start to develop sexual attraction towards each other. The boys want to date for the first time and the girls are often afraid to attempt, but some give in due to peer pressure. Friends, who have experience having sex, pressure the boys to sleep with a girl for the first time, and most give in to remain in the clique. Many take risks without thinking or using protection, and some girls become pregnant in the process. The teachings in Biology class also contribute towards boys and girls having the urge to explore what the discussions in anatomy and physiology are all about.

In this naïve state, no one thinks of the consequences of what is about to be done or what has been done.

The thought process may not be active due to lively hormones, which contribute to the decision-making process. They often make poor choices at this stage. Boys and girls have not discovered who they really are and often yield to peer pressure. It is always about what the norm is, what is trending, and keeping up with the Jones' rather than fly solo. The main and sub-groups of friends begin.

Friends can have great influence on each other at this stage. Some have advanced experiences while some are just beginners in the dating process. Allowing others to influence you negatively when you are naïve may contribute to the beginning of downward slopes in your journey in life.

The naïve state is a fragile one, especially when you are just beginning to find your ground and have no idea who you are.

It is often more about going with the flow without thoroughly thinking, and having others suggest what to do as well as what steps to take.

I call this state "the exploration state." You have the notion to try something you have never done before. For example, you may try a cigarette, venture into having sex, explore lesbianism or "gayness" and so on. If you are in any way connected to your spirituality, you may hear your inner voice (the Spirit of God in you) tell you not to act on these urges, but because you are curious at this stage, you are tempted to dive into adventuring and this may be the very beginning of your painful journey in life.

Your First Attempt

Juggling schoolwork and social life in high school can be tough. You have to deal with the teachers and the assignments. Some of the male teachers cannot even take their eyes off you and you begin to struggle with coping in class.

If you attend an all girls' school, you may not have exposure to so much of the opposite sex. The boys often came around after school hours, and hung out in front of the all-girls schools in order to check out girls and start a relationship with them (if they can finally do the convincing). As a girl, your girlfriends influence you to go on a date with the boy in the picture. That is where it all begins. The boy's friends, on the other hand, influence him to give up his virginity and convince the girl to do the same.

Most boys know how to organize the parties that lead to the girls giving up their virginity; all in the name of what they think is love. One of them volunteer to hold the party at his place while his parents are at work or out of town. They may also find a club to hang out at, or it may be at the mall. Nowadays, things happen in awkward places. People have sex in the bathrooms, in the parking lot, at the park or at the library. If at the house, these children organize easily. They usually have someone watching the door and driveway for parents, while those involved in sex take to the room. If, as a parent, you have not had the sex talk with your child yet, it may be too late as they may be starting to discover what sex is all about. (Do not hesitate to share your journey and experiences to help your children understand the real deal.)

Sometimes sex happens this way, while others give up and walk away, showing that they are not ready to explore sex. There were several attempts made by John, in order to be with Leslie, but she kept resisting due to the morals instilled in her while growing up. Every time they held hands, her mother's voice would echo in her heart and she would quickly excuse herself and return home from school. John had made a bet with his friends that he could convince Leslie to have sex with him, but she never gave in. At some point, he forced himself on her by kissing her and grabbing hold of her breasts. She resisted and pushed him off. That was the last time they saw each other. Leslie decided she was going to stick to the morals her mother had imbued in her. She was committed to saving herself until she got married.

Not many girls can be as brave as Leslie was. They give in due to peer pressure and the eagerness to explore something they had never experienced before. They listened to stories friends told and made their decisions based on someone else's lifestyle and choice, which came with consequences.

Not knowing who you truly are and what your purpose is during the exploration phase may lead you to become inquisitive and to experiment sexually. It may also be the beginning of looking for love in the wrong places.

Looking for Love in the Wrong Places

Helen had watched her parents fight day after day and night after night. Sometimes her dad would leave and not return until a day or two later. She watched the neighbor console her mom occasionally. He (her dad) would kiss her

(Helen) on the forehead and tell her, "Everything will be all right with time." She never experienced what love was all about, growing up with her parents. She had just graduated from high school and received admission into the college of her choice; it was her first time away from home. It was not as if she was sheltered, but she was an introvert. She kept mostly to herself due to the family situation. She did not want her friends to know anything about what was happening with her parents. She never invited her friends to hang out at her home. She preferred to meet up at their respective homes and spend time with them there. Sometimes, it ended up in sleepovers.

Helen had just moved to her own apartment, which she shared with two of her friends' off-campus. It was the first weekend in her new environment. She had no plans to go home to visit her parents and grandmother. She wanted to experience what it was like living alone. Some of the boys in her faculty had invited her to a party, but she was not sure about attending. After deliberating for about two hours, she finally decided to go. It was her first party as a college student (freshman). She had no idea what to expect. A handsome, tall man who she had been staring at all night introduced himself. He handed her a glass of wine and sat her down at a table in the far right corner of the hall. They chatted for a while and in between, he refilled her glass of wine. She got intoxicated without thinking about the number of glasses she drank. Enchanted by this "prince charming," who seemed to be delighted to spend the evening with her, she thought, *this could not be happening*. Could it be love at first sight? In truth, she had no idea who she was with that night. The party ended and Joel escorted her back to her apartment. He offered to help her get in since she was tipsy. He assisted her with opening the door and helped get her into her bedroom. The apartment was empty as her friends were not around. Joel seized the opportunity of being alone with Helen, kissing her and caressing her. Helen was drunk, the kiss took her, and she felt good at that moment. Before she knew what was going on, they had sex. It happened spontaneously, but it was due to her being intoxicated. Joel used the opportunity of serving her several glasses of wine to get into Helen's space and rob her of her virginity. She also made herself vulnerable by allowing herself to be consumed by his looks and words without paying attention to his actions.

Helen woke up in the morning to find herself undressed and under the comforter. She could not remember what happened the previous night but found a note from Joel on her nightstand, thanking her for their time together. She tried to recall how she had gotten herself into the situation. She had not planned to sleep with Joel. All she wanted was have a good time, not to lose her virginity. She felt disappointed in herself. She could not believe she allowed it to happen by getting drunk. She was looking for love at the wrong place and time.

She got up to freshen up, sat down, and started to think in order to recall what exactly had happened. She did not have Joel's number or any other information. There was no way to get in touch with him. She had compromised who she was for the looks she saw, and thought she fell in love in that moment. Where would she start? She had no idea Joel was not a student on campus. She called around to ask the people who invited her to the party if they knew Joel, but no one seemed to be able to help her. Torn as she was, inside out, she cried her eyes out after she got back to her apartment from making the inquiries. Her co-occupants had gone home for the weekend. She was alone and did not have anyone to discuss the situation with. She decided she could not let anyone hear about what had happened to her.

She kept her head up to attend lectures, but broke down every time she returned to her room at the apartment. Day after day, night after night, Helen would stay up crying and wondering what resulted in her compromising and getting drunk. She lived with regrets from that very night. She was not sure if he had used protection. She decided to get herself checked out by her doctor in order to ensure she had not gotten pregnant. As she waited for the results of her test, her heart raced with anxiety and kept her up all night.

Being an introvert helped Helen keep the situation under control. Her roommates had no idea anything had happened to her. She visited her parents but never talked to them about what had happened at the party. Early one day, Helen got up to visit her doctor in order to obtain the pregnancy test result. Her pregnancy test turned out negative. She felt relieved and continued living her life while keeping silent about what she had experienced. Everything seemed to be going okay in her final year in college, until she fell ill prior to completing her thesis and rushed to the hospital. She was experiencing chronic stomach pain, was always fatigued and had noticed her eyes suddenly became yellow. Little did Helen know that she had actually contracted Hepatitis B the night she slept with Joel. She had no symptoms whatsoever until a year and a half after the incident, but the virus had begun to damage her liver.

How could this be happening? This was not what she had planned. This was not how she envisaged her life would turn out. She had felt unloved as a child; her parents fought and she watched quietly, which tore her apart, but she never spoke about it. She had bottled up a lot until she met Joel. That night, he listened to her and gave her all the attention she had been missing.

Helen had let her guard down. She gave in to drinking with him. She was entangled by his sweet, manipulative words. She did not realize they would end up sleeping with each other, or that she would never know who he really was and may never cross paths again. Here she was, lying in a hospital bed with a disease gradually taking a toll on her life and eating her up.

Some of us today, like Helen, do not take the time to think about what we are getting into during our teenage years. We think of things as trends: it is in vogue, it is the norm so we have to participate. We allow society and culture define how we should live. We hold on to the thought of, *"Everyone is doing it, so why can't I?"* This is how you start looking for love in the wrong places.

We forget about who we are, why God created us, our purpose/mission and lose ourselves in the exploration process in our journey.

The Exploration Phase

The exploration phase of our journey allows us to start to discover who we are, but most of the time, we are not aware of this; hence, the reason why most of us get lost in the process. This stage, as a teenager, is where you start to become aware of yourself, your hormonal changes, and body changes. Attraction towards the opposite sex and interest in sex develop at this time.

The exploration phase is where all the desires, ego, fear, pretense and so on begin to come to the surface. At this phase, each individual begins to crave to experience things that you are yet to explore. The need to fit in with society in order to be accepted begins to creep in. You start wanting to dress up like them and act like everyone else around you without realizing that you were created and designed for a unique purpose by God.

The ability to connect to your spirituality at an early age can make a huge difference during the exploration phase. On the other hand, when you do not connect to God or have not developed a personal relationship with Him, you will continue your journey in the exploration phase, which may lead to easy or painful paths depending on how much of yourself you truly know at this stage. Fitting into society, culture, tradition, yielding to peer pressure or trying to impress and please others, oftentimes more than not, results in getting lost further. The ability to reason on your own while weighing all your options will help you decide if you want to conform to the worldly standards and accept what society is offering, or decide on your own which way to go. The decisions you make will have a great impact on the life you live.

The exploration phase is also, where you may start to make friends and develop associations that can either help shape or break you during the teenage years. Association is always because of the desire to belong to a well-known group or trying to fit into a particular group in order to gain recognition.

Seeking recognition due to fear of being rejected by others often results in losing oneself a step further during the exploration phase.

NUGGET 2

Before God Formed You

The Unique You

Prior to your conception in your mother's womb, God knew you. He was the One who created you. He had the knowledge of who you will be and become. He created you in a unique way that is different from that of anyone else on earth. God matched up everything He used for your creation so that you can stand out from everyone else. He created you in His image and after His likeness. He also equipped you with everything you will need to survive from birth to death: your ability to cry, laugh, sneeze, breathe, sleep, wake up, think, hear and eat. God put together all of these in your sensory nerves and in your brain when He created you *complete*.

Your mother carried you in the womb for nine months where you learned to swim your way around, suck (for some), eat, sleep and swallow, amongst other tricks you tried out while in there. God knew everything you would be and become before he let you out of the womb. From your first cry after birth to your first smile, God knew all of these.

The day you were born was epic. You had been incubated for up to nine months. The excitement about your arrival gave everyone an adrenaline rush and the news of your birth quickly spread to friends and family members who were dying to get a glimpse of you and hold you in their arms.

Your making was not just something orchestrated by your parents; it was all part of the Creator's plan. He knew you were significant and you were going to have an impact on those who came into your life at any point in time throughout your existence on earth.

You were not just another template. He chose to make you different for a reason. He never designed you to be like anyone else. He gave you a destiny to stand out and be the UNIQUE YOU. He wrote your story and handed you the script, letting you know it was time for you to start your journey. The journey to discovering who you are on your own. No one else can walk the journey God created for you. You will have to decide whom you will bring on board to play the different parts. He, however, knows about everyone you will come across and all those that will be part of your story and journey in life.

> *The reason why God singled you out of the crowd and made you "perfectly imperfect" and uniquely "you" is because no one else can be and is like you.*

You were made *"perfectly imperfect"* because you had flaws that would help you learn about who you really are and cause you to learn and grow in the process. Each flaw has a purpose and a time to serve you. You just have to learn how to identify what the lessons are and how you will utilize and apply them towards your growth.

Getting to Know You

From baby bottles to diaper changes, you learned to cry when you needed food or to have your diaper changed. It was your first response to anything that would get you attention. You knew if you cried, someone, if not your mother, would be right there to attend to you. You had your game plan on right from your earliest stages. Yes, crying will get you whatever you want at the right time. It was how you got your needs of eating and changing your wet diapers accomplished. Smart little you! You started to figure out things early on in life.

Now that you had mastered how to call attention to yourself, you started to learn the little ways of manipulating others to get the attention you needed when you needed it. You could raise a false alarm by crying to get the attention of your mother, grandmother, father, grandfather, uncles, aunties, siblings and other family members. After all, you were the latest addition who needed all the tender loving care. However, this may not have lasted for as long as you wanted it to. You realized they soon started to leave you to cry for a while. You intensified your cry a little louder so they could hear and become worried about you. "What could be wrong?" would be the thoughts running through their brains, just to get to you, pick you up, rock you, check to see if your diaper is wet and now they seemed to be getting the hang of your false alarms by deciding to let you cry a little longer. This trick did not last for too long, you must have started to figure out. Therefore, you devised another little scheme.

You started to smile so you could have their attention. Friends and family members carried you once you wore that smile on your face, making everyone realize how cute you are. They just wanted to hold adorable you. You responded with your facial expressions and little coos. You had now learned to delight in attention seeking.

You were able to accomplish these things by learning to process your thoughts towards getting what you need, now. You were getting on with your exploration phase and becoming better at it. Now that you thought you had it under control, it was time to begin to relax, but unfortunately, it was just the beginning of your journey to discovering yourself in terms of how you perceive yourself, not necessarily the "you" God created you to be and become.

You later on learned to feed and fend for yourself. You started as early as learning to crawl and became frustrated sometimes when you could not seem to figure things out. The early discovery of you may not have seemed to help; you realize the need to connect back to your spirituality (and to God), especially if you have no one around to lay the foundation for you and in you. You may sometimes have had the foundation and noted connect to God because you were following your self-will.

Your parents may have tried to talk to you as much as possible, but as a teenager, you always had the urge to venture out on your own to learn new things, which may sometimes have gotten you into trouble or helped you learn how to get out of trouble. You had just begun to get to know yourself by taking risks and adventuring into doing things all by yourself. This adventuring stage can lead to mixing with the right people, or the wrong people.

The "Conditioned You"

Growing up came with the conditioning from teachings of parents, teachers, families and culture. You were taught family foundations and traditions. You watched others around you. Your parents and their relationship gave you some ideas about what love is, as well as other couples, either dating or married, that you were acquainted with or grew up around.

The school routines, the family traditions and cultures, the talks we had with family members and friends all had a part in the conditioning of our beliefs and set the pace for how we live at this phase of our lives. These stages set the stage for you to discover who you are, why you are here and what your purpose on earth is. However, we do not realize this yet. We are just beginning to get our feet wet with what we think is reality, but is not necessarily actual reality. We become passionate about some of these things and continue our journeys of self-discovery and exploration. I will talk more on this later on in the book.

The Right and Wrong Mix

Teenage years and high school days are the beginning of the experimenting phase in one's journey. You come across two kinds of "mixes": the right and wrong mixes. The right mix includes those who choose not to go with the flow. They understand what it means to stand out. They have their own cliques, but refuse to fit in with the popular group. They stay positive without looking for trouble, but rather building into each other, and strive to achieve the very best academically.

The wrong mix is the group of teenagers and young adults who always want to be "in the know" or become famous. This group may consists of children who had a painful childhood experience (due to situations in the family, a parent on drugs, an abusive parent, family background, or their neighborhood) or who are currently experiencing a painful situation and feel neglected or rejected. In order to gain acceptance, they may exhibit bad behavior, which only yields negative consequences. Making decisions at this early stage requires critical thinking skills.

The wrong mix may get you into smoking, drinking, drugs and sex. It may be a combination of one or more of these. Drinking, smoking, doing drugs or sex takes your focus off your academics and help you connect to physical/fleshy desires that satisfy in the moment but do not help you think or focus on the future. You forget who you are once you start mixing with the wrong crowd. You forget the reason you are here and your purpose. You lose yourself completely in these things. You become consumed by any of them. Some people have lost their lives by getting involved with the wrong mix.

Eric and Jack had been friends since elementary school. They attended the same middle school and were now in the same class in high school. Eric had always wanted to be amongst the popular boys in school. He thought it was cool to be a member of the group and at the same time be famous. This group got away with a lot after school hours and sometimes would get into trouble during school hours with teachers and the principal. Eric made away with a lot, in the midst of the group, due to Jack looking out for him and giving him a heads up before they were recognized. Eric continued to get into the wrong mix after leaving high school and while attending college.

The day the course of Eric's life changed forever lives in his memory. It was a summer night and there was a party off college campus. Eric had stayed at school during summer to take some classes. He was supposed to be studying, yet decided to attend a party his drinking "buddies" had invited him to.

Eric was getting ready when he started having the gut feeling not to go along for the party. However, he decided to go with his friends. They left the party at 4 a.m. the next morning. They all had too much to drink and the driver was highly intoxicated. None of them thought about the amount of alcohol they consumed that night. The driver was speeding and eventually lost control of the car.

The driver made a sharp turn around a tight corner of a ramp; the car somersaulted about five times before eventually landing in the ditch off the ramp. Eric was the only survivor of the tragedy. He was in the hospital for several months due to broken limbs and fractured ribs. Luckily, the accident did not result in his paralysis. After his recovery, he became sober.

Mixing with the wrong crowd led Eric to the point of almost losing his life. He had lost his mother at an early age and that left him devastated. His father had re-married but his stepmother treated him badly. His father defended the stepmother always, which made him feel unloved and resulted in his negative behavior.

Eric made poor choices instead of seeking help. His father had no idea how torn Eric was on the inside. During his therapy sessions after his discharge, Eric started receiving counseling to help him recover from the accident, as well as the death of his mother.

Not everyone is as fortunate as Eric is. He survived. It almost cost him his life before he finally got it right. Are you struggling with a similar situation? Do not wait before it is too late to get the professional help you need. Do not wait until your life starts to go down before speaking up. Drinking, smoking, drugs and sex are all distractions that draw you away from your purpose in life. They move you towards self-will. Some end up becoming addicted once engaged with drinking, smoking or sex. These things also contribute to the deterioration of one's health. Pause for a moment and think about the diseases associated with smoking, drinking and sex. Diseases range from liver disease and cancer to AIDS, just to mention a few. Most of these diseases have no cure, if you think about it and digest the thought. Why waste your life when you can live it to the fullest? Becoming involved with drinking, smoking and sex often starts as an experiment.

Surrounding yourself with the right friends that look for the best in you, as well as bring the best out of you, is key to walking the path towards fulfilling your purpose in life.

The Experimenting Phase

The experimenting phase is one in which you have to be extremely cautious of the choices you make. These choices can lead you, or they can break you. The inability to determine which is best can be critical in life. The experimenting phase is a bit chaotic for a teenager. This is because he or she has not yet completely learned to discern what is right from wrong.

The teenager has just begun a process of learning how to figure things out on their own, and this includes decision-making as well as the ability to think critically. Some will get frustrated at this stage and want to quit, feeling discouraged and worried about failure. Fear starts to creep in during the experimenting phase and if care is not taken, it occupies a huge space in one's journey.

Lola and TJ met in high school and started dating. Dele had some friends who were no longer virgins. Having listened to their stories, he engaged in watching porn with two of his friends. He started to hang out with them to watch more and more porn videos. This led him to start masturbating. His friend Richard had told him it was not a big deal, but it was all about discovering manhood at age 16. Richard lived with his grandmother, who was always working. Serving in the military resulted in his parents' deployment. The more TJ spent time watching porn, the more he developed the urge to have sex with Lola.

Lola, on the other hand, was a naïve young girl. She had promised to keep her virginity until she got married. TJ, however, kept putting pressure on her to try it. He would kiss her and fondle her nipples to arouse her. She struggled to pull herself away, even though she enjoyed his touch. She decided to talk to her friends about it, as she happened to be an only child whose mother worked two jobs in order for them to live a good life. Lola lost her father just before her birth. When she talked to her friends, she was surprised to discover that most of them were no longer virgins. This made her curious and she decided to experiment since she was "in love" with TJ.

The following day, Lola and TJ met up after school hours as usual. They hung out at Richard's house to do some homework and spend time together. Her mother was not going to be home until late at night, so she could afford to spend time with TJ at Richard's place. Richard left them together in his bedroom, while signaling to TJ to get things moving. TJ did not waste time. He unzipped Lola's dress and started to caress her nipples. This sent sensations down her body and aroused her. She tried so hard to resist but her body was yearning for more.

She whispered to TJ to be very gentle with her and they ended up having sex that evening. When it ended, her heart sunk. Her mind raced asking herself, "What did I just do?" She could not believe she had just broken the promise she had made to herself and her mother. They did not use any protection. She wondered what would happen if she got pregnant? What would happen if she found out TJ had a sexually transmitted disease (STD)? What would her mother say if she found out?

Lola got dressed quickly and told TJ she needed to go home. He walked her to the bus stop and watched the bus drive off. He felt he had accomplished a goal. He had moved up to the level of "no-longer-virgins." He went back to share his experience with Richard, who was thrilled to see that TJ had "manned up." A month later, Lola found out she was pregnant and had to leave school to take care of the pregnancy, as she could no longer cope with studying. She had decided she wanted to keep the baby, even though TJ had pleaded with her to terminate it.

Lola's mother was extremely disappointed to see that her daughter had comprised her standards resulting in a complete turn in her life. She had to quit school as she ended up on bed rest at seven months into the pregnancy. A night of experimenting had changed the course of her life. TJ could not believe what had happened and did not support Lola keeping the pregnancy. He did not want anything to affect his studies or progress. He had begged her to abort the child before her mother found out.

His attitude had suddenly changed and he no longer wanted to have any contact with Lola. She had to struggle through it all. She got a part-time job at the grocery store where she worked after school hours until she was placed on bed rest due to high blood pressure, also known as preeclampsia. Lola's plans for college had to be postponed.

The experimenting phase helps you learn to resist temptations and learn how to overcome situations that will lead you to compromise who you are with what others offer you.

> *Not everyone will realize the reason for this phase until it is over and have gained enough knowledge to help pave way for their future or learn how their lives can take a turn from a positive direction and come to a halt for the time being.*

Not everyone experiences sex during this experimentation phase. Some decide not to venture into having sex, but still get into the wrong relationships due to either dating the wrong kind of people or having a mindset that is not flexible. You may have an unrealistic stereotype in what you are looking for in a partner. This phase involves investigating and learning to decipher wrong from right as well as learning new methods of getting things done. It also involves making decisions that can shape or break you. In some of the next chapters, we will be looking at situations and scenarios that take place during the experimenting phase.

 NUGGET 3

The Journey Begins

The Learning You

Lisa enjoyed hanging out with Dave in high school. They met after school at the entrance and spent time hanging out with each other at the mall on weekends. Dave spoke highly of Lisa to his friends when they came over to his house. Dave knew Lisa was the girl of his dreams right from high school. They kept in touch while in college and spent some time together when home from college.

Dave was busy making plans. He thought this was the beginning of a new life with her. He had plans to surprise her by proposing and was busy making plans for dinner at a restaurant where he would make it happen. Little did Dave know that Lisa had starting dating someone she met in college. She never talked about it, so Dave had no idea there was someone else in the picture. He had his eyes fixed on Lisa, a woman, who back in his high school days was a girl he admired and fell in love. She was his prom night date.

Everything about Lisa seemed right to him; the only thing that separated them was college. She had to move from North Carolina to Pennsylvania to attend school. She met John in her sophomore year in college and they got along pretty well. John and Lisa had been together now for three years and she was looking forward to introducing him to her family and friends during the Thanksgiving break.

Lisa had kept her relationship private since she had always been an introvert. Some of her friends knew about her and John, but did not have a clue of what went on with their relationship. No one had anything to say or gossip about, only that John and Lisa were dating and people knew them as a couple on campus. Lisa had accepted Dave's invite to dinner.

She invited John to come along, knowing that some of her old friends would be attending and it will be a good opportunity for her to introduce John. As she waited for John to arrive, she got a text from Dave notifying her to ensure she looked good for the event. She thought to herself, "Could it be that someone important is going to be there…a teacher, an old friend or a celebrity?" She shrugged her shoulders and changed her mind about what to wear. As she finished freshening up, she heard John pull up into the driveway. They were all set and ready to go.

As they arrived at the venue, Dave's sister, Sharon, stood by the door looking worried. She knew about Dave's plan, but on seeing Lisa with John, she felt disappointed. She was not too sure of what was going on with Lisa, but seeing her with another man left Sharon with a dampened feeling. She kept her composure and welcomed them as they all walked back into the restaurant. The evening was going smoothly and as planned. Suddenly, Dave walked towards Lisa, fell on one knee and brought out a box containing an engagement ring. Lisa looked gob-smacked! What in the world was Dave thinking? They had not even talked about having a serious relationship. What made him want to propose all of a sudden?

Dave never made his intentions known to Lisa. They were never intimate, based on their faith. They, however, were very close. This still did not equate to letting Lisa know how much he cared about her and what his intentions were. Lisa, on the other hand, had always waited for Dave to say something. She liked him but she grew up with the teaching of waiting for a man to make the first moves.

With that in mind, Lisa started dating John soon after he asked her out. She and John had some things in common. They could complete each other's statements. John felt Lisa was his missing part and could not be away from her for so long. He knew the moment he set his eyes on Lisa, that she was the woman who would be his bride. He made his intentions known to her from the very start.

Lisa felt embarrassed and assisted Dave in getting off his knees. She whispered to him and called out for John. They both led Dave aside to speak with him, letting him know that they were dating and committed to each other. Dave nodded and walked away towards his car. He opened the door, sat down and placed his head on the wheel in disappointment.

Dave realized he had never shown Lisa how much he cared. He felt heartbroken. If only he had known, she wanted to hear him say the words. Dave had just begun to learn what a difference it could make if he expressed himself instead of making assumptions. Making assumptions can lead to hurt and pain.

Without communicating with your partner, you will never know what is on their mind or obtain a response to your thoughts. No one is a mind reader.

You always have to remember that you cannot read someone's mind. Dave, in this instance, assumed that his friendship with Lisa meant that they were in a relationship, especially since they had known each other for so long. Lisa expected Dave to make his feelings known, but it never happened. This was her reason for moving on and into a new relationship. Dave was left broken. He had figured it all out by himself without getting her involved. This was just the beginning of his learning process.

Assumptions ruin relationships and oftentimes leave the one assuming in a lonely place. It also makes the relationship one-sided since there is no form of communication or agreement between both parties.

Dave had to learn the hard way. It must have been a very painful experience for him. He did not make his feelings known to Lisa. He assumed that since they liked each other, they were already together. He had teased her from time to time, but never told her he loved her. Their friendship grew gradually and deeply. Dave was not strong or bold enough to express his love early in the game. Lisa felt that since he was not communicating well, it was time for her to move on, which she did in college.

Do not wait too long before letting someone know you love him or her. You will end up losing the one you love to someone else. It is always good to express yourself, even though you may fear rejection. Rejection is not a sign of weakness, as most people think it is. Instead, it is a sign of growth when you still have more things to learn about relationships. It is much better if rejection happens earlier than later on, when it only creates more hurt, pain and a mess.

Rejection

Dave felt rejected by Lisa. It was not done intentionally, but all due to his inability to express himself. If he had spoken up and let Lisa in on how he felt about her, the relationship could or could not have continued. It may seem like rejection, but sometimes it is better to remain friends with certain people than to actually be in a relationship with them. You may feel it would have been great to be dating or in courtship with a particular person, but it may turn out to be more of a nightmare than a relationship you both enjoy. It is better to leave some friendships the way they are. Feeling rejected may initially tear you apart, but realizing that you need to learn the lessons associated without allowing your emotions to take total control is the best way to overcome it.

> *Rejection often leaves the one rejected broken. When rejected in a relationship, it affects a person's emotions, ego and self-esteem.*

If the affected party is not strong enough, rejection can be extremely damaging, lowering esteem and raising ego in defense of fear of failure. In the case where you held back your feelings, you contributed to your rejection. The one who rejected you may have felt you were not ready or that they needed to move on. Their season in your life was over, though the friendship may still exist, but not as strong as it initially was.

Rejection may also be due to a break-up. Your relationship may have ended on a sour note rather than friendly terms. You may feel all alone and confused when this happens. You may sometimes try to convince the other party to allow you to work things out. Doing so will lower your self-esteem further than it was before. Realizing that there is a time and season for everything that happens in life is a quicker way to start moving on and forward. It may seem easier said than done, but the reality is that people will always come and go in our lives.

We cannot force anyone to stay. People come into our lives to teach us what we need to know about ourselves in order for us to grow – to become better, not bitter. To build your esteem back requires positive reassurances. Know that **you are good enough** when God created you but not ready or good enough for the one who rejected you. Take time to think of what went wrong and right in that relationship and document the lessons learned. Work on yourself and do not be so quick to jump into another relationship. Take time to heal and accept yourself more before venturing forward. Rejection from one person does not mean you cannot find love again...so do not be too hard on yourself. The one meant for you will always be yours, no matter what!

Is It Just Attraction?

Dave was attracted to Lisa, but she may not have necessarily been into him. Dave felt rejected by Lisa. There is a huge difference in becoming attracted or being attracted and being compatible with someone. We oftentimes mix the two up and these result in one party feeling frustrated.

Knowing this early on in the game can help you realize that some relationships may just be based on attraction and are going nowhere, compared to those based on compatibility that may be heading towards marriage. Relationships should not be for play dates but for finding someone who will complement the other and work towards marriage and procreation.

When you initially meet someone, attraction is what happens first. Fascination may be due to the looks, the physique or the charisma used to catch your attention, but oftentimes, you forget about everything else. The attraction grows as communication progresses. The more communication flows, the more you will discover if you both are compatible or not.

> *One reason why most relationships do not delve into compatibility earlier on is that both parties become infatuated due to attraction and mistake it for love.*

Another reason is that while two people are infatuated with each other, lust slips in and both become carried away by the lust instead of thinking about the important issues of why they are coming together. Infatuation and lust are often mistaken for love, but are far from what love really is. These cannot help you know what love is, especially if you do not yet know who you are.

Break-ups

Every relationship that did not work out, was not meant to be, or it was not the appropriate time, should you end up coming back together in the future. We should learn to say thank-you to the "ex" when a relationship ends. You may think I am crazy making such a statement, but the truth is, we did learn some lessons during the worst or best times we had while in the relationship. Hence, we should thank our exes for making us realize that we needed to grow in those areas brought to our attention. It is the truth, but it may sound bitter, just so you can be better.

We oftentimes think break-ups are bad. We make them sound like life-threatening surgeries that we can never recover from. The reason we feel so much pain from breakups is that we connect to our emotions, which make us feel we are not done yet but we can still recover the relationship. Emotions, fear, hurt, pain and anger all rise when a break-up happens. We forget that compassionate side of us that would do anything to make sure the other partner is happy. Hurt and pain may sometimes make us forget about who we truly are and become who we are not when we put our energy into fanning the flame of pain rather than healing from it. Some become angry because of the break-up. The thought of being alone does not resound well for some. They cry and reminisce for days without thinking of what good will result from the break-up, instead focusing on why the other partner decided to exit. Engaging in sexual acts, more oftentimes than not, make break-ups more difficult to handle. This is due to soul ties created during sexual intercourse.

Sex and Soul Ties

Have you ever wondered about soul ties? Soul ties are associated with sexual relationships. You often create a soul tie with someone you have sex with casually or randomly. Yes, sex connects to the soul and it can be hard to untie until you seek for the person's peace and free yourself from it. Have you ever thought about someone you had sex with a long time ago (I am talking about years ago – way back then) when feeling lonely or craving to be in someone's arms? You may be in a relationship or marriage and still reminisce about a previous relationship where the sex was great and you keep finding yourself going back there in your head. The way to break such ties is to seek and make peace with the ex.

> *Sex is a powerful way of connecting to the wrong people and can leave a negative effect on you when you meet the right person due to previous soul-ties.*

Think about the silent diseases that can be acquired during such relationships (some not curable and some acquired even with the use of condoms). Saving yourself for the "right person" may save you from connecting soulfully to someone else. You may say what if the "*right one*" is not good in bed? In that case, you can always teach your partner what you enjoy and you both can get down and learn together, as long as you are both willing to give it a shot. (This may be the reason why some people or relationships are messy.)

Attractions, breakups, rejection and soul ties all occur during the learning phase. The learning phase of the relationship is the beginning of the journey to discovering who you are and what your purpose is. In the process of becoming attracted to someone, you may end up getting infatuated, which is often mistaken for love (you will learn about this in another nugget), then experience rejection or be involved in soul ties. All these are part of growth in order to become the real you God created you to be.

Tying your soul to the wrong partner may become a difficult bond to break without having to grow through a lot of pain. When your soul is tied to someone, your emotions run on high. You develop separation anxiety when the relationship ends. To untie your soul requires seeking for the partner's forgiveness just for the sake of your own peace. Never choose to tie your soul to that of someone else. You will be hurt and become broken completely.

Knowing and understanding your partner is very important in any relationship. Once you get to know your partner, you will know what to do in terms of accepting to be in the relationship or waiting for the right person to show up. We will be looking at the different kinds of people we may come across while in the dating game in the next nugget.

NUGGET 4

Understanding the Characters

Who They Are...

We sometimes enter relationships without taking the time to know or understand the other person involved. You start by becoming attracted to the other person and initially become infatuated as you spend more time together. The more time you spend together, the more you can learn about each other. However, the mistake some make is that instead of learning about their partner, they allow their emotions to take the driver's seat. When emotions come to play, the opportunity to learn about the partner is lost. You were so enticed by the attraction-emotion process that asking questions does not seem to come to mind.

You may also not have figured out who you are, and this often leads you to seeking for "wants" in others rather than looking for those missing pieces of the puzzle to finding you. The missing pieces to the puzzle will help you discover what you need in order to feel and become complete. Sometimes what we need is what we seek for in others, but until we find it within ourselves, we will keep getting hurt. This is how we will come to learn and begin to grow.

The ability to decipher your partner's character from the beginning of the relationship will help you determine if you both are *compatible*, have *chemistry* and *complement* each other. These are the big three "C"s of any relationship leading to marriage.

> *The three "C"s ~ Chemistry, Compatibility and Complement ~ should be the deal-breakers or makers for you when looking for a partner in a relationship.*

How many values do you share? How well do you know and understand each other? How compatible are you? How well do you complement each other? Are you spiritually connected? Do you know his/her background, family or medical history? It is essential to know your partner's family history, medical background, do's and don'ts, vision and dreams, interests and career. It is also important to know how you fit into the picture in his/her life, as well as them knowing these things about you. Not asking questions early enough leaves you with assumptions and speculations that contribute to the destruction of relationships.

Lola did not know TJ that well. They hung out and got involved with lust in the process. She had no idea he would insist on her getting rid of the pregnancy. She thought he loved her, but apparently, neither of them really understood the meaning of love. It was infatuation and lust, and that seemed to have expired the moment Lola found out she was expecting their child.

How many of us go into relationships thinking that everything will just work out without us having to do some work? We get eager to be with someone, but do not take the time to find out about that person or check him or her out with others who know him or her well. We have an idea of what we want but not necessarily what we need, as we ourselves have not taken the time to soul-search and figure out who we are and what we need to make us feel complete prior to bringing someone else into the picture.

Lola was eager to be with TJ. She did not check him out or ask questions about his future, his present, his family and so on. What would happen if TJ were HIV-positive? What would happen if he had STDs (sexually transmitted diseases)? What would happen if he were hypertensive or diabetic? She did not know or ask about any of these. She had no idea about his family history or background. You may think this is not necessary, but it all adds up to the character of your partner.

We sometimes overlook these areas and forget that childhood experiences do affect people in a way, and without knowing, you may never know how to handle situations you will face when living together. Not every partner opens up about their past, but you want to ensure that you know as much as possible before the relationship gets deeper. You want to make sure you know how you can help your partner heal should he or she have previously experienced abuse or had a painful childhood.

You will come across many different characters when you start dating. You have to be able to understand these characters and see how they fit into your goals and can complement you before you decide with whom to settle down. You may not realize it is necessary at first, and that is why you become so broken if the relationship does not work out and you seem to have put so much into it while it lasted. The next few nuggets will introduce us to some characters we may come across while dating.

The Female Narcissist

The female narcissist is all about physical appearance. She loves to dress defiantly, showing off her assets in order to attract the males. She is very vain with a focus mainly on outward appearances – her hair, makeup, shoes and clothes – while paying lots of attention to her looks. She believes no other woman is as good-looking or as good as, she is. She spends money mostly on brand names. She may also spend money on plastic surgery to enhance her looks.

She is usually an attention-seeker who also enjoys taking and posting pictures of herself on social media in order to attract the opposite sex. She is a socialite who likes to make a significant entry at social events. She believes she is special, famous, and successful. The female narcissist is spiteful and overly confident. She always looks for opportunities to talk down on others, and feels that others are resentful of her. She always expects others to dance to her tune. She does not sympathize with other people and is quick to exploit them. She likes to compete with others.

Female narcissists are quick to blame others for any problem they face and are very arrogant as well as impatient. Quick to make excuses for her shortcomings, these women will lie to get what they want and are very dishonest. A female narcissist likes to engage in risky behaviors and acts out frequently. She exhibits mood swings and cannot decide what she wants to do. She is quick to defend her irrational behaviors. You will, not know initially, that you are dating a female narcissist – until she entraps you.

If you are not ready to embrace the lies, manipulation, control and abuse, then do not attempt to date or marry a female narcissist.

The Male Narcissist

You had no idea what you were in for when you met each other. His stylish dressing and clean look attracted you to him. He seemed very nice and caught your attention, but the conversations seemed to be one-sided at the very beginning. He talked much about himself, sharing his pathetic stories in a way that got you to connect with him.

It seemed like you were not understanding him or listening attentively. He would cut you off and interrupt you, dominating the conversation, but you let it slide; after all, you are a good listener so why not listen to understand. He clouds your world at the beginning of the relationship and constantly seeks attention while at the same time talks about his accomplishments and goals/visions. It almost makes you think you are in a lost world, but the attention seeking is just to tie you down so you cannot focus on anything other than him.

The narcissist hardly talks about his friends or family and is constantly talking down on others. He makes it seem as if not everyone cares about him. Everyone is leaving him all alone to make things out on his own (the somewhat immature and sympathy seeking trait). When dating an egocentric narcissist, you will have to reassure him constantly of the relationship you have. He is usually captivated with entertainment and entertaining others. For him, entertainment is to seek for acceptance and domination of others.

He may have emerged from a fragmented family and will not talk or seek help about it. You will always feel like you are an add-on for certain times of convenience but never really in a relationship like the one you truly deserve. For the male narcissist, the relationship is often long-distance and they prefer to keep you at arm's length rather than close proximity so you will not figure him out too quickly. Sometimes, he prefers dating married women just because a relationship with anyone single may appear serious and he is never willing to make a commitment.

He sometimes claims to be or tends to appear as a workaholic just to make it seem like he is always busy. Short-term relationships are usually the plan, so that once he ends with the first person, he moves on to the next victim to exploit. He will lie about anything and everything to get what he wants from you.

He likes to lead and be in control all the time. He will argue to the point of winning always. Never try to argue with a male narcissist; you will only end up feeling hurt or broken, thereby lowering your self-esteem gradually until you start to feel hopeless. He does not know how to love or be compassionate. It has nothing to do with you; that is just the way he is and has become mentally shaped. If you happen to come across one who wants to go on a date or have a relationship, be mindful of the following signs:

- He is excessively charming towards the opposite sex. Women are usually attracted to him due to his charismatic nature.
- He usually appears very confident and thinks about himself.
- He constantly talks down on others.
- He likes to brag about everything.
- He loves to show off and hold lavish parties just to get the attention of others and to be in control.
- He appears to seem to want to save others, but it is all part of his antics.
- He is insecure and needs constant reassurance.
- He sulks and acts like a child when criticized.
- He does not care about your feelings and always puts himself first.
- He expects you to constantly adore or praise him.
- He expects you to be there for him but he will never be there for you.
- You always have to make him feel special due to his fragile self-esteem.

- He always thinks that others admire him and are jealous of him and his accomplishments.
- He never sees himself as wrong but always right.
- He usually likes to take advantage of others for his selfish gain and wants the best of everything for himself.
- He is very materialistic and is always engrossed with his outward appearance.
- He is unfaithful, manipulative and controlling. This can lead to him becoming abusive.
- He will break you and leave you more badly hurt than you bargained for. Staying in such a relationship will leave you lonely.

It is worth knowing that no one is born a narcissist, but the attitude/behavior develops over time through painful pasts or childhood memories that your partner has refused to deal with, instead shut off, and locked up. Without dealing with these issues, the narcissistic tendencies double in no time.

The Shady Partner

The shady partner is usually in a relationship for what he or she can get rather than give. Everything about them is shady. Some of them are players and you cannot get them to speak the truth. They like to manipulate, seduce and pretend just to keep you in the relationship and keep it going. They always have something to hide and you cannot get them to tell you what it is, no matter how much you try.

Most of the time, they get into a relationship with an agenda only known to them. They may also get some of their friends and family to play along so that they can accomplish their mission.

The shady partner tends to gather a lot of information about you at the beginning of the relationship, which they usually use as a weapon of blackmail towards the end. This is how they tie you down to them. This kind of partner is quick to run to your family and friends for support when you try to call off the relationship. This may be because he or she is no longer receiving any more benefits from you for their own good, not necessarily yours.

> *If you do not know who you are, you will end up sympathizing and staying with the shady partner yet fail to see that they have an agenda to accomplish.*

You may feel threatened by the shady partner, which may lead you to stay in the relationship. This is often due to insecurity this kind of partner is experiencing or may have experienced.

The Player

The player is a man or woman of sweet words. They can easily woo you and sweep you off your feet within the first few hours of conversing with them. The player's main motive is to get you in bed just to satisfy his/her temporary pleasures. Players can be manipulative or quiet rollers who gradually sneak into your life in order to win you over. These people have been either previously hurt from a broken relationship or have carried childhood experiences along without seeking help or taking the time to heal.

The player often looks for sex as a means of soothing pain. This usually happens at the peak of when they think they need to feel loved. In most cases, they find those who are vulnerable and caring or have been through a similar situation that will reason with them. This way they can share their story and obtain sympathy from the other party.

Once a player gets your initial attention, they will not stop until they get your full, undivided attention. They call you frequently in order to get into your space and get you to start showing you care. They immediately secure that space and win your heart over. The moment you give in to having sex, they become eager, move in and close out.

The deal is sealed and you may never hear back from them. If you attempt to call afterwards, they may never answer your call or will come up with excuses letting you know they will no longer be available. You are once again left broken. I would encourage you to refer to my book *Love, Sex, Lies and Reality* to learn more about the player.

The type of partners discussed in this nugget are the ones you will often meet when you are not too sure of who you truly are or have been broken and have not taken the time to heal, recover and become refined. At some point in time, you may have met some of those described above and you may feel confused, wondering why you keep meeting the wrong people. It just means that it is about time you get to know you!

NUGGET 5

Who Am I?

Finding the Real You

You have to take that journey to truly find yourself, in order to know the real you God created. Life experiences (never call them mistakes) help you through this process of discovering the real you God created you to be.

> *You may sometimes have to experience hurt/pain in order to discover yourself. Other times, pleasant situations will lead you to who you are.*

You may have to lose the self you know in order to find yourself, the way God created you to be. When you experience hurt or pain, ask yourself, "What is in it for me?" Do not focus so much on the painful experience. Let the hurt and pain lead you to soul-searching. Think about what led you to the point where you actually experienced the pain.

Imagine having a cut or bruise. Trace the steps that led to you getting cut or bruised. Only then, can you truly learn and understand the lessons in the hurt. Pain is sometimes good. It helps you grow. Never resist it. Never deny it. Never run from it, but learn from it. When you learn from it, you will be able to identify with it, realize what was in it for you, prevent it from re-occurring in the future and embrace it in the moment, knowing the lessons in it were valuable to you and will help you in preparing for what lies ahead.

Yetty was broken several times during her college years but she resorted to staying celibate and taking some time off dating. She found it hard to believe that she had not thought about seeing or dating someone in six months. The thought of being with a man never occurred to her. She felt okay being all by herself. After a while, she decided to join several singles groups on social media to see if she would meet anyone.

Unknowingly to her, it was just the beginning of hurt/pain. She met Ben and he was all over here. She felt blown away by him and thought that all the sweet words he uttered were filled with meaning. After three months of being together, Ben started to pester her to give in to sex and she thought giving in to the relationship, after he constantly spoke of his plans to introduce her to his family, would help their relationship become stronger. She did everything she could to make him happy, especially after he lost his job. She spent every dime she had on him with the hope of him getting a job in the near future.

Yetty had no idea that Ben was a player and that he had played many women on social media. He had no plans for Yetty. Two weeks after they had sex, she did not hear from him again. She had tried calling him and had visited his place, where they often met. His friend notified her that the apartment was not Ben's but his. He only gave Ben his keys so that when he went out of town, his apartment would not look vacant. Wow! She had no idea Ben did not own the apartment. His friend told her Ben still lived with his parents.

She had no idea where he stayed or had that much information about him. "How did I get myself to this place?" Yetty asked. She thought she had met the man of her dreams, only to find out that a player had pranked her. Her stomach churned and she felt like throwing up. How had she allowed her emotions to rule over her decisions? Ben was obviously a sweet-talker.

Yetty felt torn apart. This was her third experience. She longed for love but ended up chasing after lust. This brought her to her soul-searching journey of discovering what went wrong in all those relationships. What was she doing wrong that led to her repeating the same mistakes? Some of you may be going through this now, but have not yet connected the dots back to you. What you are longing to find in someone else is what leads you to repeating the same patterns, which result in lust and eventually heartbreak.

Yetty had to soul-search after going through the painful experiences that left her hurt and broken. She realized that the issue was not with the men she invited into her life, but due mainly to what she accepted and conformed to that resulted in her getting broken. If she had stood up and refused all offers brought to the table without having to give in to feel accepted, none of what she was experiencing now would have happened. She was not patient enough to wait for the right time.

The process of her finding herself will require her to begin with soul-searching.

Begin Soul Searching

No one can do it but you...

> *Until you come to realize who you truly are and own your situation, you will keep getting hurt and feel rejected in any relationship you enter.*

Others may try to help you while being patient with you, but the reality is, NO one can help you get there or change you until you are ready to take that step. You will only keep inflicting more pain on yourself when you let your ego ride, and you keep on fighting yourself while trying to manipulate, hurt and use others in the process.

Doing this hurts those that love and care about you, but the one who gets hurt most is you, and in the process, you lose blessings and miss opportunities. Learn to seek solitude and soul-search. Take time to address every single pain you have carried, heal, and forgive yourself and those who hurt you. Let those circumstances serve as opportunities for growth instead of holding on to the pain and becoming bitter and resentful. Do not hold on to grudges and strife that serve no purpose but result in much more hurt and pain.

There is so much more you can achieve and enjoy when you take the time to accept every lesson learned, heal, forgive, discover yourself and move on in newness. Your very best still lies ahead, once you move beyond the past hurts and pain.

The soul-searching process should take you back to the very beginning of your life's journey. Where did the pain start? Did you have a terrible childhood? Were there any family fights you witnessed that tore you apart a bit?

No matter what you may have been through, you will need to take a deep dive back to help you heal completely.

Touch on every pain that you may have experienced. Ask yourself the question, "What did I learn from it?" not, "Why did I have to go through it?" We will always wonder, but it is better to leave some things best untouched. When touched, they cannot ease the pain but instead inflict more pain. This is the reason you have to move beyond the "why" to the "what" questions. During the soul-searching phase, you will need to clear out all thoughts and the mindset that you previously had in order to be able to absorb the truth, as things start to unfold and become clearer to you.

Yetty had been broken several times in the past. She, however, did not take the time to heal but kept looking for love in the wrong places. She felt she needed to find someone who would love her, but she usually ended up in the wrong arms. She fell for sweet words repeatedly. She was usually in a rush to be with someone. She never took the time to address her needs and figure out why she kept meeting the wrong people until she decided to soul-search.

She wondered and started to journal about all she had been through in her journey. She did this on a daily basis for about a month and was finally able to start to come to terms with all the experiences she gained (never call them mistakes; they are part of what leads to your growth and finding yourself in life). She was now able to see the reason why she needed to soul-search and prevent herself from getting hurt in the future.

It was a simple situation turned complex, but now with soul-searching and moving towards a new life, things will begin to change for Yetty.

Soul-searching often brings out the obvious that you ignored and opens to light the lies that you may have told yourself in past years. The fear created as illusions may also surface at this stage. Fear is an illusion we create that limits us from stepping outside our comfort zone. We may not really want to deep-dive into soul-searching due to issues or situations we may have buried and do not want to resurrect, but the reality is, if we do not address these issues, we may never resolve conflicts that arise. It is good practice to uncover any hidden issues, which result in breakdowns or conflicts. You will be able to resolve them once you figure out what they are.

During this process, I encourage you to journal as much as you can. Doing this will allow you to note every single experience in detail. Leaving out information at this phase will only hurt us later on. I had to keep a journal, which I eventually burnt once I was able to make peace with everyone in my write-ups. It is necessary to make sure that no event is undocumented. Leaving out events only awakens the hurt and the pain if not properly handled now.

> *Learn to lose the self that you are comfortable with, in order to find the self that you truly are and were created to be.*

Dealing With the Results of Soul-Searching

Soul-searching results come in five different stages:

The awareness stage, the angry stage, the crying and laughter stages, the release stage and the separation-anxiety stage.

The Awareness Stage

The awareness phase is "brought to light" through soul-searching, but you do not necessarily begin to heal until it starts to really sink in deep. You realize you were part of the equation. You did contribute by letting yourself think you could give in and win your partner over to get what you wanted (temporarily) but not necessarily what you needed long-term. You gave in because you thought you could convince them to change. You now realize you could not do anything; you can only control you and are only responsible for you. Your heart may sink and you may wonder why you allowed all this to happen without thinking it through. Do not feel bad about what you cannot control; it is all in the past at this stage. This is your journey to the new you, your journey to healing. Hang on and hold on tight.

Darkness emerges and turns into light at this stage. You may start to become aware of some of the things that happened to you in the past or from childhood and can now tie the knots together and realize it is all coming together and making sense. This is the awakening stage of your journey in life.

> *This is the beginning of your discovery of what your purpose really is. This is your 'aha' moment of realization that you had been living in a trap and you are lost and need to get it all back together.*

This is when you realize you cannot control anything in your life.

It seems a bright light just ran through you. You have just gone through a full virus scan and the awareness wakens you to see everything in the light of truth. You may start to experience some of the following at this phase:

- Issues that you have buried for a long time are now, coming to light and awareness.
- Revelations of instances you previously ignored.
- Old, unhealthy habits are being revealed.
- You realize that ego had been at play in some instances and prevented you from owning up to your moments.
- It all seems scary and real.
- Old relationships and occurrences during the time you spent together are coming to mind.
- The lessons you ignored are all resurfacing.
- You start to run low on energy as memories from the past flow in.
- You suddenly feel overwhelmed by the truth revealed.

The Angry Stage

You are beginning to be filled with rage now that you have become aware of all you gave in to. You are mad that you let yourself down. You are mad that you let someone else take advantage of your weak points, and you gave your all, yet now you are the one hurting.

Yes, I know how you feel. I have been down that lane before. I gave it my best – my very best – and I was hurt in the process of trying to please someone else because I did not really know who I was and did not love myself enough. The next stage will help you let it all out.

Ego starts to struggle to retain its place in your progress in order to hold you back and keep you right where you currently are. Your defenses are awakened to make you feel you did not do anything wrong, and you are struggling between embracing the truth and holding on to the façade. Negative thoughts are all that you can think about at this stage.

If care is not taken, this stage is where you can go all out on a revenge spree. Players usually halt at this stage instead of progressing in life's journey. They go on to plan strategies they will use in playing at others – this can be done subconsciously because ego is dominating and dictating the pace of things. Ego makes the player feel that defeat is not acceptable, but for him/her to succeed, it has to be on vengeful terms. Everything done at this stage happens with ego and fear at play.

This stage can also lead you to become humble and at the same time angry with yourself for making poor choices. This stage, for some, will be the "I own my mistakes" moment, while for others, it leads them to further life destruction steps and away from finding whom they really are.

The Crying Stage

Your anger has led you to feel stupid. Why did it have to happen to you? You have unanswered questions. The tears are rushing down and out. "Oh, why me?" you may ask.

The tears flood your eyes, you feel drained, and you lay awake all night, wondering and pondering. The expectations have resulted in complete disappointment. You feel completely used.

> *Let all the tears out, let all the pain out, let all the steam out. Yes, you need to cry, sob, and do whatever it will take.*

I felt this same way. I would stay up all night. I questioned God several times until I realized He had nothing to do with it but it had everything to do with me. I gave in to all of this. I had not listened to the still, small voice while He gave me all the warning signs. Some of them I took lightly while ignoring the spirit within me, giving me all the alerts and flags. I cried for days until I realized it was my entire emotional bank running out and I had to learn to become strong. I became fully aware of my mistakes. I was responsible in part for giving myself to hurt and pain. I know better now. I have become wiser now. You can do the same. Learn all the lessons and ensure you document them at this stage.

Facing this stage made me realize how disconnected I was from God, even though I knew who He is and had a relationship with Him. I was not tuned to my spirit man (the Holy Spirit, given to me right from my creation). I cried until there was nothing left to cry for. This was the beginning of my release phase and facing the reality of who I truly am. It was the end of the questioning season of who I really was and the beginning of the phase of the real me.

The Release Stage

This is the beginning of the forgiveness phase in your journey. You have emptied out most, if not all, of your anger, hurt and pain. You feel sober and blank. Wow! You may say to yourself, "Did I really allow myself to go through all of that?" You may laugh at all the stupid things you have put yourself through for nothing...absolutely no reason for them to happen!

There will be moments of laughter and moments of tears, and that is very much okay. It is all for good reasons of growth.

Let me share my personal story with you. During my process of soul-searching and dealing with results, I was up sometimes in the middle of the night as I found it hard to sleep. I had worked during the day from home struggling to pull through the eight hours. I was supposed to be tired at night, but that was when I had all the energy to stay awake to soul-search. I would have my dialogues with God and I would reminisce for a while.

My discoveries sometimes made me feel stupid. I thought to myself, *"Did I really do that?"* I would laugh, I would cry, and sometimes I would sit in complete silence.

I had to laugh at myself after crying sometimes, in the middle of the night. I had mixed and flooded memories dating back to my early teenage years and discovered how I had repeated the same patterns. The release stage allowed me to bond with my spirit and let go of all the hurt/pain, emotions and memories that were not worth holding on to.

Looking back now, I see how naïve I was in the way I handled some issues, but I know better now. The discoveries were quite a revelation.

The silly things we do sometimes for love without realizing who we are can be amusing. We may try to deny it, but soul-searching brings them to light. Such musings will forever remain in the archives.

I learned to release the memories that I had held on to from childhood and never talked about. I became aware that holding on to all of these memories resulted in me repeating the same patterns and getting into the wrong type of relationships over and over again. I realized I was connecting sympathetically instead of focusing on empathy.

There were days I stayed up all night as I had flashbacks – many flashbacks – of all the hurt and pain. I had to let go. Now that I have become aware, I realize I contributed subconsciously and unconsciously. Sympathy may lead to hurt, but empathy will allow you to connect to the right person without connecting to their pain or past. Pain draws us to those who are hurting, and that is usually because of lack of awareness or ignorance on our own part. This is why soul-searching is very important for release, forgiveness and healing.

The soul-searching process can result in the shedding of tears, since it uncovers a lot of the self-denying we have done right up until this very moment. How many lies we have told ourselves and now can reveal everything before our very own eyes. What were we thinking? Why did we wait this long to discover all these things? Why did we let ourselves go through it all up until now? It is the "**eureka**" moment. It is magical. It is unveiling! Yes, we finally realize all the time we wasted doing things we could have learned from earlier on. Alas, the *"aha" moment*!

There is no need for regrets at this point. Yes, it may seem like years wasted, but the reality is that the lessons came at the right time when you needed them most. The lessons learned from your journey so far are to help you face the present and future. It may take a while to digest everything, but I encourage you to take time to slowly digest and absorb what you have learned from soul-searching.

> *Once you have obtained the results of soul-searching, there will be no way you would want to go back to those things you did back then.*

You now realize where you made mistakes and you know never to do the same thing again. Although we are still vulnerable, we must definitely remember the lessons when dating or planning to re-marry.

Does this mean that there are no more lessons to learn? Absolutely not! There will always be lessons, as long as we are living and growing. We learn every day. God actually speaks to us through everything around us – from the ants, storing up their food in the summer and working together as a community, to the roses that thrive amongst the thorns and bloom so pretty. The birds are able to sing, reminding us that there is a song for every season and phase we go through.

Learning never stops, but making good use of the lessons we learn from each experience along our journey is vital to our growth in life. Everyone grows, but not everyone becomes mature. We only become mature after we have gone through the necessary processes that help shape and tame who we are to be in line with the real person God created us to be. Only then can we truly realize that we were "created" **complete** right from the inception of the world. Next comes the learning to forgive.

The Separation-Anxiety Stage

The separation-anxiety stage is that stage where all the adrenaline and guilty feelings start to rush back at you. You may have those whom you are planning to forgive show up and try to make you feel guilty while blaming you for their pain. You have to realize that you are not responsible for anyone's pain or healing process. You are only responsible for yours. Your role is to forgive them and move on in newness.

Never take the blame for anyone else's decisions. The guilty feelings will only hold you back if you allow them to limit you to your comfort zone of pain. You are stronger than you think you are and it will take you pushing through with faith to overcome.

Release all that is holding you back, and be determined to move forward without holding on to painful memories.

> *Trees do not hold on to dead leaves but make room for new ones to grow. You cannot hold on to pain and think healing will come.*

You have to let go of pain. Receive your healing and live in newness, knowing your very best lies ahead of you.

Let me share with you how I faced this stage. I had released everything and I started to get phone calls that made it seem like everything that had happened was my fault. Guilty feelings began to overwhelm me and I started to relapse back into the angry stage. I wanted to heal but the pain tried to keep me feeling like it was my fault that everything had happened. I cried out to God night after night without sleep and tears filling my eyes. Then, I heard God say to me the words, "My Grace is sufficient." At that point, I knew I had to pull myself together and fight the thoughts; they were all because of illusions in my mind.

I started to recite affirmations throughout each day, and these helped me stay focused, even though I still had the thoughts. My determination to heal was what I held on to, and I pushed harder. Allowing positive thoughts to overshadow negative ones with affirmations is vital to moving to the forgiveness stage. It is a struggle, but you can absolutely do it. Stay focused, stay on track and keep pushing hard. **Let your faith take you to where your fears cannot chase you. You are stronger than you know!**

Learning to Forgive

Learning to forgive those who hurt us, is one of the most difficult phases we go through prior to healing. Although it seems like part of healing, it must occur prior to the healing process.

The first thing that comes to mind is the question, "Why do I have to forgive someone who hurt me?" Forgiveness frees you from the guilt that eats you up without you knowing – guilt of failure, fear and disappointment. No one wants to feel like a failure, but things happen that we just cannot control and do not have control over. Once you forgive yourself, it is easy to forgive others by letting them know and making peace with them. Forgiveness is vital to moving forward and freeing oneself from bitterness, anger, rage, malice and strife, which only grow roots of hatred and not love.

Remember, love covers all wrongs and the moment you choose to love, you must be willing to forgive always and let love overshadow everything else. Forgiveness is for the one hurting, not for those who hurt you. Forgiveness is not for those who hurt us, but for us to heal completely and obtain peace, knowing that we are free from that situation.

The moment we let them know we forgive them for hurting us, we are able to feel relief. Over the next few days, you will discover the pain no longer exists.

The reason we experience so much pain is that we tie our emotions to the pain, sometimes due to soul ties created from the relationships. In cases of soul ties, forgiveness unties your soul from those you previously had sexual relationships with. The memory is no longer tainting, but it gradually fades away. You will no longer feel angry or hurt, but can look back and laugh at how silly you were when such a relationship existed.

Going about forgiveness in a subtle way is essential to the healing process. You must discard any form of anger, bitterness, resentment or strife at this stage.

> *The purpose of soul-searching is to become free of every form of pain, and the purpose of forgiving those that hurt you is to free you completely from anger, malice, bitterness, resentment and strife.*

To begin the forgiveness process, identify everyone you need to forgive by creating a list. The earliest event is where you will begin. Now that you have created a list, the next step is to start by setting up a face-to-face interview with each person. This may seem difficult, but know that it is very doable. It is not confrontation, but more like intervention to free yourself and your soul from any ties or form of pain, anger, resentment or strife that you may be holding on to. I suggest you hold back your tears as much as possible. Shedding tears will get you emotional and make it hard to break the ties. Part of soul-searching is freeing yourself through forgiveness.

Another point to note is that not everyone will accept your forgiveness, but you have to remember that you are doing it for you and not them. You are freeing yourself from them. You have to stick to the goal, even if they respond inappropriately. Your inner peace is more important at this stage, so there will be no need for getting into an argument or going back and forth on a discussion. Listen as much as possible, and do not try to get even with the conversations.

Do not let it seem like you are bringing yourself low to let them know you have forgiven them, or like you are asking for forgiveness. The purpose of forgiving them should be your focus. Once you have completed this phase, this leads you to the healing process.

For those you may not come across due to inability to reach/contact them, take a sheet of paper and write down the words you would share with them if you had the opportunity to talk to them face-to-face. Read your paragraphs/sentences back to yourself. Find a place outside of your home where you can burn the sheet(s) of paper as a sign of eliminating that picture or that season from your memory. You can also decide to shred it after reading to free yourself from the past so that you can move forward. Whichever way you choose, you must let it all out and let it go. Let God heal you as He has forgiven you.

Starting to Heal

Clearing and de-cluttering your mind through forgiveness removes the pain you have endured for so long. The hurt you experienced held you back, telling you never to forgive those that hurt you, but the only one who bled during those days was you. Now that it is over, it is time to start to heal. The healing process involves seeking inner peace. Inner peace begins with connecting with your spirituality and finding your way back to God. It may be difficult at first, especially since you are trying to pull yourself together. A dialogue here or there will do it, for starters.

As days go by, you will need to reaffirm yourself with every memory of pain that comes up by telling yourself you are healed and free from the pain. The healing process purifies you of negativity and guides you to focus only on the positive thoughts. This is the beginning of your shift.

Remember this: there can be no shifting until you are ready to shift ~ moving from your pain through healing towards your purpose.

Your healing process results in your freedom from pain. It allows you to redefine your goals and is the beginning of self-love realignment.

I have had to walk through the process of forgiveness. It takes you back to places you do not want to visit, but when you come to realize no one benefits from seeking for forgiveness other than you, it becomes an easier task to handle than you initially thought.

 NUGGET 6

The Healing Process

Pain is a form of denial and fear. It is self-inflicted illusions that reign in place of truth. Pain holds you back from seeing God's truth about your existence. It is a denial that His love for you is unreal when in truth. God's love is so real. It is your thoughts that cause you pain. Thoughts couple with emotional hype, resulting in pain and feelings of rejection. You refuse to accept defeat; hence, you stay held back in pain due to fear. Nothing but the thoughts that you hold on to inflicts pain on you. No one else gets hurt but you in the long run. God did not give fear, but love: *"For God has not given us the spirit of fear, but of power and of love and of a sound mind"* (1 Timothy 1:7).

For you to be able to move forward, you must release all fears and pain that are holding you back from progressing. Every experience in life serves to make you grow, not causes you to become fearful.

Releasing Fear

When you approach the healing phase, fear of things changing from what you are comfortable doing may start to creep in. Many guilty pleasures start to arise and make you think you are about to take a plunge into the sea of no return. The reality is that fear wants you to give in and give up.

Fear of abandonment or rejection is very common in a relationship (and with the self). Being committed to someone requires taking risks and becoming vulnerable to some extent. However, the pain of a previous breakup may prevent you from wanting to get too involved, and thus, you become defensive. If you tend to become afraid of loving someone due to past pain, you may never be ready to enter a relationship. Take time to heal from the past relationship, love and rediscover yourself, focus on the lessons learned, and be willing to love again. When you have healed, it will be easier to embrace and accept love when it comes. The right relationship will always make you feel safe, even if there is still some amount of fear left in you. You will be able to feel closely connected to the right partner while maintaining your individuality, honoring, loving and accepting each other fully well.

> *Fear is an illusion that we create within our thoughts that limits us from stepping outside our comfort zone.*

The reason we are addressing fear at this stage of the healing process is that fear usually is a showstopper for many and it may become difficult for you to move beyond this point and receive complete healing. The most common form of fear that may hold you back is the fear of what others think. You do not want to seem to hurt anyone, yet you need to heal. When these kinds of thoughts surface is when you need to summon the courage to begin your healing process.

Fear is a form of illusion that often deludes you from the truth. It makes you want to believe it is the truth, but there are no facts to it. Fear is a way of relying on your own strength instead of relying on God for strength. It makes you want to hold on it deceitfully, and allows you to become anxious and develop panic attacks. You always want to believe you have control of a situation due to previous hurts and pain that have led you to believe you have failed. You begin to trust in yourself and your own strength by believing you can find solutions on your own without any help or even allowing God to step in. Fear makes you worry, become depressed, wallow in sorrow, become angry and think irrationally.

We cannot achieve anything on our own; that is why we have to return to God when we fail or learn the difficult way through life experiences. God is and will always be our source of strength, and we should learn to trust Him for this. The strength of God in us is what allows us to achieve many things in life and become successful doing so. We have to realize we are frail and we cannot fix our mistakes. We must become aware and allow our confidence and faith in God to draw us closer to Him for help, rather than remain in denial and delusion.

> *Healing requires daily affirmation of your truth. Healing requires your connection with "the now" and refusal to focus on the past.*

The painful past will strive to work its way into your memory, especially when you come across anyone who takes you back there with talks.

You may find yourself trying to relate to what you hear someone say, and reenact the scenes in your thoughts. You must be determined to let go of the past by reminding yourself that nothing you do can change it. You can only hold on to the lessons learned and ensure you do not work backwards but press on forward.

The more you practice daily affirmations of positivity and speaking life to yourself, the more you find the healing process working in your favor by removing fearful thoughts.

Dealing with Ego

Ego is awakened by fear, and as part of the healing process, when we suppress fear; the ego tries to remind us of the facades that were once in place. Ego rises as a form of defense against fear. It serves as a reminder of the past. Ego shows up as a means of defense when we are guilty of sin or wrongdoing. Ego does not want you to look at the wrongdoings or sinful nature; rather, it allows you to pretend as if the problems never happened. It does not allow you to evaluate the wrongdoings and work towards resolving what led to them. Instead, it tries to hold you back. With ego comes the "what if" questions.

Ego, when defensive, is coupled with fear; hence, the "what if" questions. "What if he/she finds out the truth?" Ego always has a mapped-out plan of denials and lies to be told to cover up the wrongdoings. It works at making it seem the wrongdoings never happened, rather than allowing you to become aware of the situation and rectifying things. Ego is an illusion of self-defense, with the need to cover up and lie about every wrong done. The more it shows up, the more lies the individual tells. The more lies are told, the harder it becomes to face reality. Ego can lead to self-destruction if you don't take care.

You have to remind yourself, just as with fear, that you no longer live in the past but you are on the verge of moving forward, never to turn back, striving hard to accomplish what lies ahead.

Ego can also serves as an energy booster on behalf of fear by making you brag about yourself rather than dealing with the underlying issues. It makes you feel like you have everything under control when you actually do not.

The moment you start asking yourself "why" and "what if," in that very moment realize that fear and ego have clashed and are about to send you backward in time. You always have to remember the reasons you forgave yourself and those who hurt you. Doing this will prevent you from becoming captive by the thoughts stirred up by ego and fear.

> *Always remember, fear and ego are illusions created within one's thoughts, and all they do is limit you to your comfort zone.*

The moment you have those thoughts, focus and channel your energy towards positive thoughts with daily affirmations. (You will find some affirmations to work with in the appendix.)

Letting Go of Self-Defense

We tend to defend ourselves against the truth. We do not want others to see our weaknesses, but the reality is that defense serves as a form of self-deception and denial. Its purpose is to hide reality, attack, and pretend that truth does not exist, or try to distort truth with lies.

Defense is a form of illusion that is birthed out of fear and ego. It is a wand that we wave unconsciously in an attempt to escape from answering anyone who tries to pry into areas we have locked away when we do not want to face the truth and own up to reality.

> *Facing the truth and owning up to reality is the only way to break down the walls of self-defense.*

BEING SINGLE

Healing cannot begin until we are ready to let go of self-defense and embrace truth and peace, eliminating that which obscures reality and holds us back from progressing.

You may have been let down, but that does not mean you have to raise self-defense mechanisms to protect yourself. God already protects you, and you sometimes have to be vulnerable, taking calculated risks, to get to where you need to be in life. Remember, love always protects. Letting go results in healing and releasing your mind and thoughts to embrace the truth that sets you free. There is no need for defense where truth lives. This is because you know who you are and know what is acceptable by you.

Your reality and truth lets you know when to work away from things that are not acceptable to you or not in line with your values.

Life is all about taking risks and making decisions. We sometimes may be hit hard and let down when we set higher expectations that are not met. This should not prevent us from forging ahead.

One of the reasons why we stay hurt or in pain is because we allow our emotions to drive and let our thoughts take the negative lane in life. You can always undo the reserve button to push past the limitations you have set within your thoughts.

A little nudge to awaken your soul sets the pace, and can change the course of the wind that will redirect you into changing your thoughts and allow your faith to rise. Be willing to step outside the box, not worrying about what anyone has to say to you or what they may think of you. Do not be afraid to fail, because failure just means you have an opportunity to succeed and soar while spreading your wings once again.

Let the fact that you have been given another chance to breathe serve as an awakening of your soul to live and fly above whatever you are facing. Remember always that life is about learning, and without learning, you cannot grow. Take that bold step of faith and step into the greatness that lies before you. You are stronger than you think you are and more powerful than you may know. Let your healing begin to flow.

Handling Doubts

Doubt is different from fear and ego, but they are all siblings born out of the illusions we create within our thoughts, inclined towards negativity and restricting us from aiming for anything outside our comfort zones.

Doubt will make you second-guess every positive thought. You begin to ask yourself, what if you cannot survive or make it on your own? You almost want to take a step back into the past. You may sometimes have thoughts of going back to your past and saying sorry all over again. The key is to know that the pain came into being so that you can move towards your purpose.

Every experience from the past leads to a brighter future. It is not always about the pain but about the processes along your journey, the ones that eventually lead you to your purpose in life.

Doubt increases during the healing process when you start to listen to other people. Listening and engaging in sharing your thoughts during your healing may lead to confusion and serve as a drawback to your healing process. Learning to shut off outside noise or outside sources during healing is key to you receiving complete healing when broken.

> *In silence lies clarity. Take moments during each day to be silent and the answers will gradually come to you as you listen to your inner voice – the Spirit of God in you – speak.*

Let Faith Arise

The healing process strengthens your faith as you connect with your spirituality and allow God to heal and touch your soul. This also will require you to own up to past situations without playing the victim all the time. The victim mentality is self-created and does not really exist. It takes two people to be in a relationship, and healing from the pain will help you believe in yourself and have faith that things will become better as you move along in life. You have come to realize you cannot do anything on your own. You need God and those whom He has planted to sow positivity into your life.

The way to create a faith awareness within you is through daily meditation and daily affirmation that will help you strive forward and push through every obstacle. This will build a foundation within you that will lift you beyond every challenge you face. The more you grow your faith, the more you are able to see obstacles on your way as stepping stones to your greatness and achieve so much more.

> *You cannot have faith when you have no hope. You cannot accept when you are not planning to receive. Keep your faith up and be hopeful. Believe, receive and achieve!*

Allowing faith to take over fear not only gives you the ability to step out of your comfort zone, it also allows you to become aware of how powerful you are. We sometimes do not realize how powerful we are when we are held back by our past pains and hurts. The "aha" moment releases and awakens the new us and we start to embrace the gifts God has endowed us with from the very start. Faith starts to push us towards purpose and we start to move into self-love, abundance and newness of our lives. It is such an amazing experience.

I could not believe how much I deprived myself of until I started to trust God more, even though I had initially thought my faith was strong. I realized I had gotten too comfortable with myself and learned to let my faith rise as I opened myself to receiving God's love.

 NUGGET 7

Self-Love

Finding Your True Identity

Your name gives you an identity, but your personality/character shows who you really are. God had everything about you written down in your book. Your book is unique to you, and no one else has your DNA or script as designed by God. It is not tied to family traits but to you as God designed and formed you – fearfully and wonderfully made (Psalm 139:14).

People know and call you by your name. However, the impact you leave on others is associated with your personality/character. Your reputation, on the other hand, has to do with what others think or believe. Your personality/character is, however, more important as this can break or make you. When you do not know who you really are, you suffer from "identity disorder."

You may be something to the world and another to those who love you and know you one-on-one, yet to yourself, you are someone entirely different. This can be detrimental to you mentally, physically and emotionally. People may perceive you as one way and, after a few weeks or months of getting close to you, begin to discover you suffer from identity disorder. Some will bring it to your attention, while others will let it slide.

You may also be in denial or may not be ready to receive it when notified. This may be because you experienced some childhood pain or went through bad experiences or relationships, and you have shut off and zoned yourself out. Until you address each hurt or pain, you will not really know who you are. You had bad experiences, and those led you into hurtful situations. You may also come up with schemes to hurt others in the process without you knowing what you are doing; your subconscious will inflict your pain on others and cause you to acquire more pain in the process.

We live in a world where culture and society have conditioned us to avoid telling each other the truth, but instead, behave as if everything is okay.

People may know that what you are giving out is wrong, but they will smile with you to make you feel good without telling you the truth to your face. It is not that they do not care, but they may have noticed that you are not someone who is willing to embrace the truth; hence, they would rather pacify you than help you heal and discover the real you. The reality is that no one can actually help you discover you but YOU, and it will not happen until you are tired of going around in circles and have had enough of the façade you have been putting up.

You may cover up with lies, fake it, or make others believe one thing, but it does not take that long for truth to manifest as revelation. The only one who gets hurt in this process is you, and this is because you are not willing to deal with reality. The moment you admit to your cover-ups, the lies, the faking it to make it, you will begin your journey to discovering the real you. Trace every step of experience (do not call them disappointments) and begin to embrace the lessons in each step.

You may have all the degrees in the world, you may have all the intellect in the world, but your character truly defines you.

Let me share a bit of information with you. I was very good at putting on a smile in the past. I was raised partly by my grandfather, who taught me so much about self-esteem and keeping my head up high all the time. When I did not have it all together, I still learned to wear a smile on my face to make it seem like everything was good. It was like applying concealer to cover my scars, but the scars did not go away. They were just temporarily covered until I washed off the makeup.

I was that girl everyone thought had it all together but I was dying on the inside. I co-led the women's prayer team. I coached and counseled. I served, but I could not discuss what was going on with anyone but God. I would occasionally ask a few questions here and there, but no one knew I was asking for myself.

I had to learn the hard way that applying makeup does not hide the scars and flaws; they will always be there anyway. It was not until a friend I was mentoring spiritually revealed her findings that I broke down to own my moment and admitted to all the pretense I had been putting up to make everything look good. I knew then I was only hurting myself in the process. I had been lying to myself all the while and now the wineskin had burst in the open.

This led me to the journey of finding my true identity. I had to own up to all the lies I told myself and make it clear that I was no longer going to lie while pretending that I had it all together. Putting up the façade was over.

> *Let your character be a true reflection of you, not the one you want the world to perceive. You will only be deceiving yourself because with time, all will be out in the open.*

The only one you will be hurting in the process is you. Learn to stay true to who you really are and apply changes where necessary. There is nothing as good as being the real you. Finding your true identity is not a one-time thing but an ongoing process of gradually learning to know who you are.

Learning to Love Yourself

Now that you have healed and forgiven yourself and every other person who may have hurt you, it is time to start loving yourself all over again. You may have in the past, but now is the time to renew, refresh, readjust and realign your thoughts and ways to focus on you and start to experience self-love.

You may ask, "How do I know if I love myself, or how do I learn to love myself?" Self-love starts with accepting yourself the way God created and designed you to be. You are a masterpiece and a work of art. God did not create anyone to be like you when He worked on you. He designed you for a purpose and you were born with love. You cannot really utilize your gifts until you know who you are and start to walk in your purpose.

Love is part of your essence. Love is part of your completeness. It just takes a few steps in finding out that you are indeed of love and love to be "loved."

Your ability to embrace your being with your flaws, your body, your looks and your entirety is the beginning of loving yourself. You recognize that what others have to say cannot define who you are and what you are. You realize that you are the determining factor to your failure or success. You alone can stop yourself from growing and going. The obstacles you face do not define you, but you are able to see them as your stepping-stones to overcoming the challenges in your way. You are able to align your thinking with God's thinking, knowing His Plans are to prosper you and not harm you (Jeremiah 29:11).

Remember that you are God's creation, made in His image and after His likeness and everything He created was good. It is not about what anyone thinks, but what God thinks about you. Loving yourself will help you understand that you alone can make choices that can transform your life or can deplete your growth.

Self-love requires your willingness to embrace constructive criticism, being open to hearing the truth and embracing it in order to grow. This will lead you to accepting those who can speak life to you and would not hesitate to tell you things as they really are. You will also begin to shut down negativity that could draw you back into self-pity or pain. There will still be pain encountered, but such has to do with you receiving and digesting the truth spoken to you.

Your existence in life is not to please anyone but God. Your existence in life is to fulfill the purpose for which God created you. Your existence in life is to share the love you are born with and made of with others so that you leave an impact on every life you come across.

Self-love helps you focus more on the lessons from each experience than on anything that is wrong or may have gone wrong. It helps you realize that it is not always about the one who hurt you but about the lessons that you have learned from all your previous experiences, which now contribute to your growth and wisdom.

> *Without the pain from the past, you will never realize the need to love yourself, change your mindset and grow to become the wiser you.*

It helps you see beyond what others see and brings you to see what God sees in you: blameless, spotless, forgiven, rescued, revived and most importantly, loved by the Master and Maker of all good things who saw you as good when He made you. It is about your abundance in the wealth of your creation.

> *Your past does not define you. Your pain does not define you. Your emotions do not define you. Your thoughts do not define you. What others think about you does not define you.*
>
> *God who made you has defined you for who you are. You are a Masterpiece made by the Master. You are one of a kind and uniquely YOU!*

You as a masterpiece came with everything you needed to survive and the starting point of your awareness in loving yourself completely just the way God designed it. You have to look deep within you. This may require you separate yourself from the noise (others, distractions, things that you are used to clinging to) in order for you to become fully aware of all you are capable of.

God created you with so much power and authority. He created you with all the positivity and energy with which you experience self-love. Yes, you are more powerful than you think you are. You are priceless. Your worth is immeasurable.

Why it took so long for you to realize this was due to all the experiences and lessons you had to learn in order to grow. We sometimes think that we face situations just for others to hurt us, but the reality and beauty of it is that we still needed to grow to become who God actually made us to be – **the real you and me**!

You had to learn to create a beautiful place of peace in your heart about the real you God worked on when He created you. Now it is time to embrace the change so that you can live. This change, due to your embracing and loving yourself, will lead you to a new place. Let the change you desire begin from inside and grow to reflect on the outside. Remember, change is a gradual process, but without taking a step towards it, there will be no change. Start with baby steps and watch the caterpillar become a butterfly.

Self-love also helps you rearrange and redefine your association with people. You will realize that you need to separate yourself from certain people and keep them at a distance. It does not mean you do not love them. It just means you cannot have them as close as you used to. You can separate yourself from people, but you cannot separate yourself from love. Love is what we are born with; love is part of whom we are.

> *Self-love sets the pace for the associations you make. The more you love yourself, the fewer unhealthy relationships you will keep.*

Self-love helps you realize your confidence is not man-given but God-given. It is not about arrogance but about learning to embrace every bit of you for who you truly are, and this helps you identify your worth and hold on to it. It also leads you to begin to realign the thoughts that help shape, make and mold who you are. You can begin to think positively without limiting yourself or becoming fearful.

We are all born with love. That which we seek, is right within us...when the time is right, the one who will complement us shows up, without demands but with love, for us to love.

When you begin to appreciate yourself for who you truly are, you will learn how to be kind and patient with yourself. You cannot expect others to be kind and patient with you when you are not doing the same to yourself. The moment you start to exhibit kindness towards yourself, the less you will allow anyone to step on your toes. You learn to set boundaries and know your limitations as well as what you will entertain. You learn to own your space, time and person.

At this stage, you also learn to protect yourself. Protecting yourself does not mean you will not be vulnerable. Instead, it means you will abide by your set standards and you are not willing to settle for anything less than those standards in place. Most of the time when we get hurt, it is because we suddenly forgot that we have set standards. This usually happens when you have not dated for a period. It seems like a long waiting period, but it does not mean you have to forget you have standards and value.

Learn to trust yourself. When you begin to trust yourself enough, you will be able to decipher the nudges from your inner spirit, especially if things do not look right about your relationship. The moment you become restless with yourself, know that something is not right. You may need to ask questions or just walk away from the situation if the answers do not tally with the vibes you have or are getting.

Do not keep a record of the past. When you truly learn to love yourself and have healed from all the pain you carried (you will still have the memories, but they do not haunt or hurt you any longer), you will let go of everything that does not serve you in any form or way. Holding on to the pain and saying that you have healed is not the same as letting go and healing completely. You have to ensure you dump everything and leave the garbage behind. It is a gradual process and you will get there with time.

> *No one is 100 percent free of garbage as we all have flaws, but you must discard painful memories that no longer serve you, if you plan to move on in newness.*

You also need to know there is no need for revenge when you truly love yourself. Seeking evil towards anyone is of no good to you. You may sometimes focus on karma, but you have to realize it is not for you to wish for anyone what you would not wish for yourself. Self-love helps you see others as you would like others to see you and to treat others the way you want to be treated.

Self-love allows you to respect others without dishonoring them. The respect and honor you give to others will come back to you when you truly love yourself. Oftentimes, when we do not love ourselves, we try to disrespect others, especially when we get ourselves into situations with higher expectations than normal. Self-love leads you to a complete vision of who you are and allows you to realize that your being and existence has nothing to do with what others think or how they feel. It is all about you, and the more you connect with your spirituality and own your life and choices, the more respect you will have for yourself and the less you will entertain those that disrespect you or have something negative to say about you.

Embracing and loving yourself also allows you to get less angry and more confident when you own up to your own mistakes, realizing they resulted from the choices you make. You learn to focus more on solutions than you do on problems. You become less boastful and more hopeful. You realize boasting or bluffing will not get work done, but actually dipping your feet into muddy waters to fish out the pearls is what helps you to progress daily.

Loving yourself lets you become more cognizant about humility. You realize everything you do requires that you stay humble and not boastful. You tend not to conform to the norm but be your own person while owning your space fully.

Love should cost nothing. The very things we seek in others are what we need to give ourselves through self-love. When we truly love ourselves, we will not seek for affection, attention or love.

Offloading

Now that you are fully aware of who you truly are and have grasped the concept of self-loving and learned to be kind, patient and appreciate yourself through self-love, it is time to offload those friends who no longer serve to add positivity to your life. By offloading, I do not mean stop being friends with them, but rather know where they stand in your life. There are different categories of friends we encounter in our journey of life. The key is to know who you need in your inner circle.

Not everyone will understand your need to offload so that you can focus on your journey and purpose, but the truth is that you do not need them to.

> *Self-love helps you determine what you need in order to keep your happiness and sanity. It allows you to choose positivity and walk in purpose.*

Distractions and noise (those whose goals/purpose do not align with yours) will only take you off the path towards living and walking in self-love, as they contribute negatively to your thought process. The dynamics of your circle of friends changes significantly, the moment you start loving yourself more. Never allow the old you to interfere with the new you when there is so much noise around you. Always remember, you cannot put old wine in a new wineskin.

Your Circle Will Change

The moment you find yourself, your circle of friends will change. You will find yourself sticking around, and to those who tell you the truth about yourself and do not necessarily get in your way of decision-making. They tell it like it is and allow you decide what you want to do when you seek their advice. You can call them any time of the day and they will be there to pick up the phone and talk to you, or better still, come over to hang out to talk. They are some of your influencers who push you towards accomplishing a lot in life (either by getting you to think or by supporting you in any possible way they can). Have at least five people in your network as part of your inner circle and as accountability partners.

There will be times to agree to disagree, but these are the people who contribute to your growth as well as help you stay on track with your purpose. Other types of friends will show up in your life, but knowing who to give an opportunity of a lifetime to is an important part of one's growth.

Once you start to love yourself, you will start to disengage from groups of friends that do not share values with you, knowing they do not have much to offer. You may still be friends with them but it will be at arm's length. Ensure you keep them out of your personal business.

Remember this:
In your weakness lies your strength,
In your brokenness lies the ability to rise and get back up,
In forgiving yourself, you find grace to forgive others,
In your healing, lies the ability to help others heal,
In loving yourself, you are able to extend love to others.

We do not have to impress anyone but ourselves. Trying to impress others signifies the need for acceptance, but when we acknowledge that God made us complete, the only One who needs to validate us is God.

Having a circle of friends who share your values will still require that you trust yourself just as you are learning or have learned to love yourself. Be in charge of your own decisions and own your journey. No one can walk it for you, and no one can achieve the goals you have set or fulfill your purpose. Self-love will lead and guide you towards taking the right steps and walking the right paths, as long as you connect with your spirituality.

Your Focus and Thinking Will Change

Now that you are connecting with the real you, the way you view things in life will change. Your focus and thinking will also change. You are more geared towards positivity than negativity. You will find yourself easily walking away from situations that do not add to you or contribute to your growth. This is normal, as you do not want to have a setback.

Your focus on your needs becomes a priority, and you are able to plan and work things out in order. Take one day at a time so you do not overwhelm yourself and return to the previous you. Thinking positively requires not projecting or setting expectations, but instead living in the now.

# NUGGET 8

My Journey So Far

How It All Began

You may be wondering why I decided to write this book. I have shared with you other people's stories and I have saved mine for last to help you understand how I got to where I am. I am not perfect and I am still a work in progress. We learn and never stop learning, as long as we are alive and breathing.

I was that naïve young girl who loved life from the very start. I had the privilege of being raised in a Christian home. My great-grandfather was a great entrepreneur and a preacher who founded the church we attended. My grandfather followed his example and so did my dad, but I observed a continuous pattern in the family. It was polygamy. No one would talk about it but it bothered me. I am that emotional child who was affected by the things I saw but never really could talk about. No one knew the thoughts and pain I had inside, as I always wore (and still wear) a smile on my face. I would sometimes put up a straight face as if nothing was wrong.

Growing up in a wealthy environment, I had no reason to complain. There were maids and chauffeurs. Everything was provided for us and we went with the flow. What else could a girl like me ask for?

My heart was however, bruised when my parents separated. My father had an affair that tore them apart and I did not see my mother for a while. The locks to the house were changed. We had to live with my grandparents for a while and we were well taken care of, but the pain of not having my mom around tore me apart on the inside. After a few years, my parents reunited, we moved back home and my mom came back to live with us, but things just did not seem the same. There was constant fighting and arguing.

There were times I was up at night and heard my parents go off at each other. It was always someone was not good enough but my mom always kept it together as if nothing happened. This broke my heart but I could not question them about any of what I heard. I was raised in a culture and at a time when children did not have the right to question their parents (and this is still the norm in many cultures). Everything I needed was provided, so why would I have a reason to complain or ask questions?

There were nights I cried myself to sleep without them knowing a thing. I would sometimes go over to my grandfather's to spend some time with him just to get away from my parents, but they had no idea why I wanted to be at grandpa's house. The void was still there.

As a teenager, I was up several nights asking God questions about why things had to happen. Why did my parents have to be this way? Why did my dad have to sleep outside the home with another woman? I would talk to my dad sometimes when I got upset but I ended up smacked and got in more trouble. I sometimes felt like an odd child for being the only one always trying to confront him with the truth. The more I did, the more he sometimes treated like me was not his daughter. We would go to church and I would silently pray with distractions raving on my mind. Why would God allow things like this to happen, especially when you are a preacher's daughter? I wondered. Why did I seem to be the only one who felt like something was not right? I continued to keep my cool and acted as if I had it together (just as my mom did), so no one knew I suffered silently. What people do not understand is that being a preacher's daughter or preacher does not stop you from temptation. It actually leaves more open doors for temptations to arise. What broke me was the affair my dad had and that separated my parents for a long while.

People often do not think of how much children are affected by their actions but I was totally not myself when I was able to add one and one together to figure out all that was going on. One of those nights when I was awake, I picked up my Bible and prayed. I asked God to show me if He was real. I wanted to know why I felt like an odd child. For the very first time, I read the story of Joseph and I could hear a whisper. It was the voice of God within saying to me, *"This is your life."* I thought to myself that it could not be; I was just reading a story and stories are not always real. Some stories are fictitious. It was just another story, but what did I care?

My heart was completely torn apart (with the feeling of rejection for always telling the truth and pain) but I had to put on a smile to make it seem everything was okay. This was the beginning of my journey of pain and hurt, but I learned how to put up a façade to make it seem like everything was great since we were not allowed to ask questions (I could not ask my mother anything). You could only talk with your parents about a few things back then. We had great times, no doubt, but I had to pretend.

> *Roses have thorns, but finding your way around the thorns is what matters in life. See the beauty beyond the pain/struggle and learn to live life to the fullest, holding your head up high...not letting ego/fear rise, and making every moment count while you still have the chance.*

I found my way of letting the roses (smiles) overshadow the pain (the thorns) I had created on the inside. I continued to push through life, keeping my head up high.

The High School Days

High school for me was great. I was that girl who was known to be a bookworm but I also socialized. I had nice, straight legs that got me to participate in fashion shows, and I represented my school. Growing up amongst my brothers and their friends also gave me exposure to how to interact with the opposite sex.

My mother embraced my brothers' friends, so our house was always packed, and I would watch to see what dating was about so that I could learn from them. I was that friendly girl, but I also knew how to put the boys in their places with my big mouth, as they called it. I was a fierce, petite girl and I always knew what I wanted and needed. I had standards and had plans to stick with them.

Attending an all-girls school also gave me the opportunity to learn from older girls who were dating at that time. They would talk about their boyfriends and I would eavesdrop to pick up a lesson or two. Sometimes I thought to myself, "Is there any reason for having a boyfriend?" I was turned off boys after listening to my parents go at each other without them knowing that I was hurting from their conversations.

Opportunities came during what we called "Literary and Society Days," when we had to go represent our high school at other schools. I was always one of the girls on the fashion runway. I could not debate, as I was shy, but I wanted to be a model as a teenager so I was able to summon the courage to parade myself during the fashion shows. After the fashion show was over, it was time to mingle and dance. The boys always wanted to dance to slow jams with a particular girl. I learned how to define the distance between us during the dance. My mother and aunt (who was a nurse matron back then) had drilled it into me that touching a boy could get one pregnant, and that fear was instilled in me, so I learned to define my territory.

I finally met a boy I liked a lot and we started talking. I had so many of them wanting to talk to me, but I was only interested in Tunde; he caught my attention and was protective of me. He was also a friend to my brothers, so that made me feel comfortable. He knew my brothers were very protective of us girls, so he always just talked with me and never really asked for anything else. We became very good friends and I started to tell him about my pain. He would console me and encourage me while reassuring me to keep my faith in God, knowing all will work out at the very end.

The Unexpected Happened

It was the final year of high school and everyone was excited. We always had beach parties and my brothers and their friends knew how to throw parties and have fun. They were all like my brothers, and we all hung out together. You could not tell the difference between us in terms of who were my parents' children.

Tunde and I continued to talk and I learned to gradually build my self-esteem. Fast-forward to summer and there was another beach party. I was always looking forward to having mad fun, as usual, but I looked out for Tunde to attend and protect me always. I had found a friend I could talk to about many of the things I was going through.

I was close to my brothers, but I did not talk much with them due to the respect I had for them from the family values we were raised with by my grandparents and parents. My brothers looked out for us girls at parties, ensuring no one messed with us.

We got to the beach and the unexpected happened: Tunde drowned, and my heart was once more shattered. I did not immediately know his death, as I had left the party for home earlier. When the boys came back, they broke the news. I was completely torn. My confidante was dead. *"How would I go on?"* I thought to myself. Whom will I share my secrets with? I had found a friend who was not like the other boys, demanding for sex, but was willing to protect and listen to me.

I could not cry in front of anyone, as no one had no idea what had just happened to me, but I would cry at night while in my bed. I would sob until my pillows got wet while holding Tunde's picture to my chest. I once again crawled into my shell for days and nights. My faith in God kept me together for a while.

Somewhere down the lane, I summoned up the courage that life had to continue and buried myself in my books until my friends started trying to match-make me, and eventually I gave in to a boy I liked (based on looks). I had no idea what I was heading into, but we always talked and I always gave him no as the answer to the reason I was not ready to have sex. My mother and aunt's words echoed loudly in my head about pregnancy, instilling fear in me and ensured I did not venture into thinking about sex. The thought of it nauseated me. My aunt headed the maternity/delivery unit so listening to her tell stories made me feel sick to my stomach about pregnancy and delivery at that stage in my life.

Life After High School

With high school over and between waiting for college results, we had time to lay back in the summer. Summer was always time to party, going from one friend's house to another. My so-called "boyfriend" was having a birthday party and wanted to show me off to his friends and family. I was ready to meet everyone, including his friends, though I already knew some of them – but hey, we had nothing else to do. I invited my friend and neighbor to go with me.

Everyone was having a great time and eventually, my boyfriend called me aside, saying he had a surprise for me. I was in the party mood and did not think it could be anything negative. It was not a time of drink spiking so there was no need to worry about that. He asked me to follow him to his parents' room to get something. I trusted him, and I was still naïve and a virgin, so I followed. We walked up to his parents' bedroom and he started searching for whatever he was looking for. He asked me to check behind the sofa to see if anything was there. I walked over and bent down to look, and I got up to tell him I found nothing.

He pushed me over to the bed, tickling me, and soon I did not find it funny any longer. I asked him what he was up to, but before I knew it, he had his father's gun in his hand and told me not to scream. I was not sure if the gun was real or loaded so I cooperated. He stripped me of my underwear and raped me. After he was done, he inserted a contraceptive pill inside me and told me I was going to be okay. I was shattered...completely broken. He called a cab for my friend and I to take us home after calming me down. I pretended to be asleep in the cab until we got home. I told my friend I was tired from partying and needed to retire. Getting inside the house, I rushed to the bathroom and took a shower. I drugged myself to sleep for three straight nights, thinking it was a nightmare. My world had completely crumbled. I never thought I would lose my virginity this way. Once again, I had to keep quiet and I put a mask on, as if everything was okay. He would still come around and I pretended as if we still had it all going great. I still would talk to him in front of our friends as if we were still together. I sometimes thought he was protecting me due to my being naïve. This was the beginning of attachment, which many confuse with love. I thought he loved me when he apologized, I did not realize it was not love. He just enjoyed the company. I was on the other hand, attached to him and infatuation was filling in. It did not take long before it died out.

At this point, I turned completely to becoming an introvert. I was no longer interested in attending parties. I was no longer interested in socializing with the boys. I turned to my Bible and started participating actively in Bible competitions. I would lie awake at night wondering why I had to go through all of these things. The pain would overwhelm me but I kept quiet during the day when around everyone else. It began to affect my studies, yet I could not really tell anyone what I had been through. From there on, I struggled silently, yet suffered on the inside.

I resulted to smoking as a way to soothe my pain, but no one knew in my family that I had begun smoking. As an asthmatic, I would smoke and wheeze. I could not talk about why I was wheezing, but had to lie that something had triggered my asthma. This continued through college for me. In college, I started adding a bit of alcohol. I began drinking champagne at night to help me fall asleep, but was never addicted or intoxicated.

I had a handful of friends that I associated with, but none of them knew what I was going through. I studied hard and kept pushing myself to make sure I did well, but sometimes I would let myself down academically when I could not concentrate. I surrounded myself with Christian friends so I could keep my faith and stay away from the boys. Unfortunately, as a young and very attractive woman, I could not keep them off, but I made friends with a number of them so I could learn what goes on in the mind of a man.

I had no idea of what healing and forgiveness were about, so I did not even think about these things. I met someone I really liked while in pre-college and church, but his mom always separated us so we remained very good friends. Having a boyfriend was not my focus at this stage, but having a friend I could talk to and confide in was what I needed. My oldest brother and I were close, but I could not tell him about my pain, especially since I felt so ashamed of myself at that time and did not want anyone to know how I had so foolishly allowed things like that happen to me.

College Years and Beyond

I eventually gave in to dating and dated someone who was my all. I thought nothing could come between us. I had it

BEING SINGLE

great when I finally met Michael, until I was heartbroken when he had to travel. His family embraced me and I was completely in love with them. They showed me so much care and now that he was traveling out of the country, I found myself feeling overwhelmed and unable to heal (all the pain came back flooding my memory). It felt like I was been rejected again. I had relied on him for so many things. Everyone knew us together. We had worked in the same hospital and it felt like we were inseparable.

I started to look for love in the wrong places. I dated someone who lied the whole time. I eventually found out that he was living with his girlfriend. The pain I had carried from my teenage years was following me virtually everywhere, without me knowing. The moment I connected with someone, he paid attention to me, listening, and giving me time, I would think, *"This is it."* I was gullible because I was seeking for attention. I wanted someone to listen to me and console me.

> *I did not realize I needed God, so I turned to man, even though I knew God, but my relationship and foundation with Him were on shaking grounds.*

I dated someone else; his family accepted me into their household, and after eight years of being together, he cheated on me. Yet again another person cheating on me. This led me to fall into the arms of someone else while looking in the wrong places for love. All these coupled

[109]

with not knowing who I was resulted in me getting myself into a situation that completely tore me apart. I was looking for a way to escape from my pain, I thought I met someone who could feel the gap and take away my pain but the truth is that two broken people cannot help each other. It will only make things worse. I tried to make it work but it just did not work out and at that point, I had to leave to keep my sanity (after 15 years), as I was very sick and stay alive for my son's sake. I cared for him, I hung in there thinking I could change things but the only thing I needed to change was the truth I withheld from myself. It was not love, it was lust mixed with infatuation and attachment attention – for deciding to walk the "prodigal" journey rather than follow, God's will. I thought I could do it all by myself even though I knew God and had a relationship with Him. It was however, not deep enough. Reality is this: it takes two people to get together and want to be with each other, but when you are naïve, you will only get yourself into a hot mess when you are not paying attention, which resulted in me holding on. Do I blame anyone? No, I blame myself for not paying

I lost myself in the process/marriage, had four back-to-back miscarriages, lost weight (I went from a size 12 to a size 2), lost five pints of blood and I thought I was going to lose my life. I had let myself down with the entire plan I had for myself without trusting God enough and following His plans for me. I also felt let down by my family when I needed them most but they made me realize this is my journey and I have to face my own consequences. I was in my final year of my Master's program and the only support

I had, was from some of the women in church who were on my prayer team, the guardian angels God sent me that I have never met (until this day), a few friends, my former co-worker, my late friend, Demola, and my son. I fought hard for my son's sake and God gave me another chance to live. This is all I choose to write about while I thank everyone from my past that helped me in one way or the other to finally connect with my purpose. You will not find me cursing or blaming anyone as this is my journey and I must own my experiences, turning each of them into lessons I have utilized to walk and live in purpose. In this way, I opened myself to see reality, deal with the lies I told myself, and embrace the truth while allowing God to work with and in me to create the real me who was conceived and born in love. As I began to heal and God kept speaking to me through the story of Joseph, I began to realize that I needed to focus on the journey to living my God-given purpose. I finally realized my purpose is to be a life and relationship coach for others; to help others move beyond their pain into purposeful living, to support them to make right choices and build healthier relationships, and to become unstuck and focus of the journey ahead. This is what led me to write my books, *Love, Sex, Lies and Reality, Being Single: A State for the Fragile Heart and another book (yet to be published)*. This also led me to start my 501c3 nonprofit organization, *Love Not Hurt Corporation,* an organization that promotes self-development and building healthier relationships (especially for those in the underserved regions of the world).

> *I share this so that you know you are not alone. We all have to go through life to find who we are and who God created us to be.*

Everything you have gone through serves as your testimony. Returning to God and love helps us to realize that God has already provided all we need. Gaining wisdom and becoming stronger while growing in faith, just as I did in my journey, is key. We always have to learn to be patient with God. Staying on God's path may seem like a challenge, but it can be extremely rewarding when we learn to wait on Him and pray.

If you are reading this and have gone through separation and divorce, do not see your ex as your pain but that phase of your life as lessons towards your growth. Life is all about growing. He/she was a layer to your growing up and preparation for the journey ahead. There is a time and season for everything. Do not hold on to a season that is over. Learn to let go and let God work on you. Realize that God has something greater that will lead you to your purpose. Focus on forgiveness, healing and the journey to purposeful living.

NUGGET 9

What to Expect Going Forward

Dating and Networking

At some point, you will start dating again. When this happens, you have to remember all that you previously learned. Think about how much self-love and trust you have experienced. You also have to focus on your needs instead of your wants.

Dating again will require that you align your values/needs with those of the partner you meet. Ask yourself, how many values do you both share? Do you both see each other heading in the same direction, five to ten years from now? Do you have chemistry?

You must be ready to accept the other party for who they are without trying to change anything about their personality. This is why it is essential to first love yourself and then focus on your values. He/she must share your values (most of them, if not all).

You must also view dating like trying on shoes at the store. If the shoes do not fit, you would not buy them. If they make you uncomfortable, you will put them down and look for a pair that will make you comfortable. View your relationships in the light of shopping for shoes. No one buys smaller-size shoes, or those that hurt while you walk. Do not just settle, but also ensure you are with someone who shares your values and complements you spiritually, emotionally and morally. When you are with such a person, you will be "equally yoked."

We often think that unequal yoke has to do with spirituality alone, but it actually has to do with emotions and morals as well. Spiritual connection must be of the utmost importance. This will help drive your faith process and spiritual growth. You have to ensure the man/woman understands where you are spiritually and he/she is on the same page about things.

> *Remember, it is not about how fast but how well you live your life. You do not want to rush into dating and get hurt again.*

You are back in the dating world. Where do you start? Finding the right mix of networking events is a good place to start when looking to date. You will not meet someone by staying at home, but by attending events that are in line with where you see yourself down the line. If you were looking to date someone at the executive level, you would not attend events where such a man/woman would not be present. Never limit yourself to places you can meet just anyone.

Be open to meeting people unexpectedly. Never judge someone by his/her appearance, either. Pay close attention to details. Words can be deceptive, but actions are often tied to the words spoken.

Meet-up groups are also a great way to meet someone. Join the groups, introduce yourself and attend events. Try online dating if you are open to that option. Always remember that dating does not necessarily mean it will lead to marriage, but every relationship comes with lessons you can learn from to build yourself up towards marriage.

Networking provides you with the opportunity to build friendships that will come with lessons. Having an open mind and attitude to learn to be friends first enlightens you and gives you a level of understanding of who the other person is. Most of the time, you learn more about people while still friends. As you know, people pretend, but within a month or two of being friends, some of their character traits will be revealed.

Networking allows you to select those you think will be a match and develop a friendship, hang out and discover who they are. Visit places you have never been to, be open to making new friends, and keep on exploring your possibilities. You will be vulnerable, but you must also learn to protect yourself. That is part of self-love. Love always protects when taking risks.

Do not date someone who exhibits traits of your father or your mother. Do not date someone who reminds you of someone in your past. Date someone who has similar values, is compatible, shares chemistry and complements you. Dating someone with the former traits is trying to relive a life that is not meant for you. You are your own being, and you need to love yourself completely to be able to love someone else in totality.

> *Never compare your date with an ex and do not look for traits that remind you of your ex; you will only be bringing your past into your present.*

Attract the Right Partner

Are you patient enough to wait? Are you meeting the right people? You can date by settling for anyone you come across to be in a relationship, but remember that it is not how fast that matters. Patience, attention to detail and learning to listen carefully will help you retain good people you come across instead of the wrong ones. You can attract anyone with your looks (and anyone can find you attractive), but you cannot allow everyone in. This is why you have standards in place. Here are some things you can do to help you attract and keep the right partner:

1. Be True to Yourself
Find the true you and connect with that. Accept your flaws and own your moments. Putting up a façade will only result in the truth coming to light over time. This will leave you hurt in the long run.

Learn to discover, accept and embrace the true you that God created you to be. Know your strengths and weaknesses. Being authentic will get you the right results.

2. Believe in Yourself
Believe in yourself. No one will believe in you when you have not attempted to do so either. Learn to trust yourself and be kind to yourself. Carry yourself in ways that reflect your beliefs and truth. Doing this will attract the right partner and help you identify the wrong ones.

3. Take Good Care of Yourself
Pamper yourself, exercise and stay healthy. Get enough sleep; groom yourself and dress appropriately. A healthy mind can only attract healthy relationships. Discard all the worries or memories of the past that you carry along when you meet someone new. Bringing your past into the present is not healthy. You will only create room for unhealthy habits while attracting unhealthy partners.

4. Be Confident in Yourself
No one wants a sloppy partner or one who lacks self-confidence. When you are confident in yourself, you are able to attract better potential partners and not settle for less than you deserve. Confidence is associated with sexiness, bringing the energy out of you. You draw attention when you walk into a room and you do not need the validation of others when you believe in yourself and feel confident. Let your confidence turn heads when you walk into the room.

5. Learn to Love Yourself

You cannot love anyone when you have not loved yourself. The first level of relationship is to be in love and to love yourself. Self-love results in you feeling more confident, believing in yourself, being the authentic you and being patient with yourself. Part of loving yourself includes owning up to your own truth, healing from any painful past, forgiving, and soul-searching to ensure there is no obstacle in your path.

6. Hold Intelligent Conversations

Having intelligent conversations will reveal a lot to you when you are seeking for a partner. Your ability to hold intelligent conversations on various topics will make your partner gravitate towards you, especially if you are like-minded. You have to be able to have these kinds of conversations frequently to figure out your compatibility.

Remember, it is your purpose, dreams and visions, compatibility and chemistry, as well complementing each other, that will determine in which direction your relationship is heading.

Pre-marital Phase

Most people want to be married, but not everyone is ready for it at the time they venture into it. Prior to marriage, you have to feel complete – not needing anyone. You must have experienced self-love and self-sufficiency, and be able to survive on your own without craving attention or longing to be in someone's arms.

You may have a close friend of the opposite sex, but you do not depend on them to be there for you. Your dependence at this point should be on God. However, do not become entangled with having conversations that make you feel you are needy. If you find yourself engaged in conversations that make you sound incomplete, needy or desperate, you are actually not ready. You need to be self-sufficient and feel complete alone, while not having the fear of being alone. If you do not feel complete or self-sufficient, I am sorry to say, but you are just not ready for marriage.

> *Take time to live, love, discover and accept yourself first. Self-love is very vital as an initial step in the pre-marital process. I hope this helps someone.*

We hope to find "the one" at some point in our lives, but the reality is that most people are not patient enough to know, understand and decipher their partners before making the bold move. We sometimes also think we can manage with a partner who is not quite right, but you must be able to tolerate the partner largely without complaining once you have accepted them as they are.

Here are some tips for those who are single and are seeking to get married or to remarry:

- If you have not fully healed from a broken relationship, do not make the move to marry someone.

Healing requires seeking solitude and addressing every area of your life. If you find yourself getting angry or upset easily, soul-search and figure out what causes you to flip or have an outburst. Discover what triggers you and what calms you down. Take deep breaths during a conversation that may heat up, and remind yourself often that you would not let anything that is not worth tinkering over bother you.

- If you are not mature enough, do not make a move to settle down. Maturity does not have to do with age but more with how you handle matters (e.g., controversial conversations, finances, etc.). You want to ensure you can handle finances, issues arising in the home, and so on.
- Your emotional age shows your level of maturity in handling matters that arise. You may be fifty and still act twenty-two. If that is the case, you are not ready for marriage.
- If you are not ready to be selfless and make sacrifices, then you may want to step back. Marriage requires sacrifice and selflessness in order for you to be able to reach a compromise with your spouse.
- Do not be overly confident in your own eyes. Humility has its rewards. Learn to remain humble while patiently waiting. Do not pretend to be who you are not when you meet anyone. Do not behave as if you have it all together. Always remember, we all have flaws and no one is perfect.
- Do not act desperate or become too demanding. It will indirectly chase someone away from you.

- Do not expect to receive every time you give, but be willing to give in love.

There are more tips than just those stated above, but those serve as a foundation before making the bold step to accept someone else into your life in order to become one.

Almost all of us want to get married, but keeping and staying in a marriage is not an easy task. It is very vital you ensure that you and your partner truly share values and love each other as individuals before loving each other as a couple and you both are ready to commit to each other till death do you part.

Checklist to Consider While Dating and Before Saying "I Do"

Here are some items you must have checked on your list before saying "I do":

Do you both share values?
Are your values the same as your partner's values? Are these values in line with your needs? Does your partner meet your standards? These are some of the questions you need to (truly) ask yourself. Do not get emotional to go into marriage, but be ready to face it knowing you are in for the right reasons.

Have you grown since you have been in your relationship?
Your relationship should help you grow, not make you compromise and feel less worthy than you have always

been. How has your relationship changed your life? Thinks and seriously consider this before venturing into marriage. Your relationship should move you forward and not backward. If you feel less confident about yourself than you did before the relationship, you may want to opt out and wait patiently for the right person to show up.

Are you on the same spiritual level?
Are you and your partner spiritually inclined, or are you just going along with the flow? Your spirituality should not change because you are in a relationship. You both should actually become spiritually stronger together. This is one of the essential things to consider when thinking of getting married. Being unequally yoked with someone who is not spiritually inclined with you will draw you back from your relationship with God and it will cost you, directly and indirectly.

When you date someone who is not on the same spiritual level with you, you will end up compromising your faith and your walk with God, and give in to what will end up breaking you.

Are you babysitting or caretaking?
Are you babysitting or acting as a caretaker? Do you have to (constantly) tell your partner what to do and how to do things, or do you both discuss and come to an agreement? Relationships are not one-sided. You both have to be there for each other. If you find yourself babysitting or caretaking, you may need to re-evaluate your relationship to make sure you are willing to do so for the rest of your lifetime together.

Do you both trust each other?
How much trust do you have for yourself as an individual? How much trust do you have for your partner? Do you both trust each other deeply? Trust is a very important part of a relationship. A relationship without trust is no relationship at all.

Prior to getting married and while courting/dating, one should have built a significant level of trust with each other. You should be able to believe your partner in every word uttered, without a doubt. You should be able to know when they mean what they say or when they are joking.

If, however, you do not trust your partner after getting married, you may want to look within and figure out if you need to address trust issues with yourself first prior to discussing it with your spouse. Trust issues may also have to do with your fears, which you will need to address personally.

> *When you choose to speak with your partner about your fears/trust issues, do so in a tone and manner that he or she will understand without arguing.*

Develop trust in each other earlier before getting married; otherwise, it may remain an issue throughout your lives together. Trust is part of the essential foundation of any relationship.

Do you truly love each other?

Love requires you to be selfless, among other things, with each other. Ensure you both love each other and it is not infatuation or lust. Lust and infatuation come with an expiration date, but love does not expire.

I have heard people say they love someone after a couple of weeks of dating. You cannot love someone that fast, but you can start to learn to know and understand him or her at that stage.

Do you both enjoy doing the same things?

You and your partner should enjoy doing things together. If you find out that your interests differ, you should make sure this would not affect your relationship after marriage. You both may become bored, or someone may get tired and venture out to cheat.

Do you accept each other's flaws?

Your partner should be able to accept you and your flaws without you having to change who you are. If you have to change to please your partner, then you may want to take a step back. A relationship should never require that you change who you are to please anyone. Learn to be true to yourself always, and the one who deserves to be with you will accept you just the way you are.

Do you communicate well with your partner?

How well do you both communicate? Are you able to resolve issues amicably without blowing off the roof? Make sure you can communicate easily and hold conversations together. Marriage is hard work and communication is key to keeping your marriage intact.

Are you compatible, and do you share chemistry?
Your partner should be a reflection of who you are. You both have to make sure you are compatible and share chemistry. Compatibility and chemistry are two essentials to consider before saying, "*I do*."

Are there warning signs you are ignoring?
You may have noticed some warning signs exhibited by your partner, but shrugged your shoulders and ignored them. Make sure you pay attention to details so that those warning signs do not come back to bite you later.

Do you know your partner's family and medical history?
Make sure you know each other's family backgrounds and medical history. This is necessary to make sure you are ready for whatever will come and can tolerate and accept things the way they are.

Bottom line: Be sure you are in your relationship for the right reasons and not just because you want to get married. Rushing into marriage with someone who is not compatible, does not share values and chemistry, or does not love and trust you can totally break you apart. Make sure communication flows easily and you can both be there for each other through thick and thin.

> *Do not be in a relationship for what you can get; rather, be in a relationship for what you both can bring to the table and share with each other willingly.*

Marriage is like a garden of roses with thorns. You have to be able to weather the storms and cross the ocean for each other always. Make it last forever by learning to wait for someone who deserves you and who you deserve to be with. Always remember, marriage is all about "till death do us part."

The Story of Ruth and Boaz

Ruth was a widow who was devoted to following her mother-in-law wherever she went. Naomi, the mother-in-law, felt Ruth was young and needed a man in her life. Ruth took Naomi's instructions and went to work in Boaz's field. She stood out. She was not like any of the other workers. Boaz noticed her because she was different. She found favor in his eyes.

Boaz was equipped with what they needed to survive. He owned the farmland/field where they met; he was an entrepreneur. His first conversation with Ruth included a prayer, after which he invited her to dine with him. Boaz gave orders that allowed Ruth to gather more from the field than she normally did.

Naomi put together a strategy, which Ruth used to approach Boaz, but he made it clear that she was a woman of noble character, not running after rich or poor men. Boaz showed respect to Ruth, not taking advantage of the moment they were alone together. He continued to show her favor and sent her back with a gift (barley) for her mother-in-law. Boaz did his research on her background and family to make sure things were clear and good to go before they got married.

You may ask, what does this have to do with you as a man or woman? A lot, in fact. Some women need to learn from this story and see that there is no need to sell yourself short and settle for just anyone.

> *Boaz knew what he needed to know. He showed respect and took care of Ruth right from the start. He even took the time to pray for her.*

Do not toss yourself at the feet of any man and beg for what you think is love. Love will never require you beg, but will show you respect and honor you.

As a single man, you need to prepare yourself and be ready for Ruth when she shows up. Do not take advantage of any woman you meet. Boaz had the opportunity to sleep with Ruth when she sat at his feet, but he did not. Learn to wait patiently so that you do not tie your soul to just any woman. He also had to check her and the family out to make sure there were no hindrances or family ties that could affect their relationship. Take the time to know and understand her, as well as her family, before deciding to walk down the aisle.

Set aside time to pray together and as individuals. Build up your faith in God through praying and meditation or quiet time in His Presence. The more you do, the easier it will be for you both to approach the throne in grace together as well as individuals when facing difficult times. As you know, marriage is not a bed of roses without thorns. The thorns are there, but you both have to push through to make your marriage bloom in every season you face.

Let love be the foundation of everything you do. Always remember, love is selfless, always trusts, and it does not keep records of wrongs. It speaks in truth and protects; it does not plot evil and is sincere. It is kind and patient. You have to learn to be all of these for each other.

Love Is Not a Transaction

> *"Love is about giving without expecting anything in return. If you have to get something back for giving, it becomes a transaction. You can only give the love you have. Love starts with self-love."*

We often think that we must give love and receive love in return, but the truth is that when you really love yourself enough, you do not have to ask for love. Instead, it is freely given to you.

You may say, "How is that possible?" Self-love is the first step to loving anyone. When you do not love yourself enough, you will keep asking your partner if he/she loves you.

Below are some pointers that will help you understand why love is freely given without expecting anything in return:

You Know How to Truly Love Yourself
Self-love involves being kind to yourself. It requires that you protect yourself from getting hurt. You have learned to trust yourself without keeping any record of wrongs from the past and seeing everyone in the light that you see yourself. You are able to tell yourself the truth without remaining in denial, even when the truth hurts and you have to face reality. You do not boost or talk down on others. You have also learned to become selfless. By becoming selfless, you are able to give without expecting a return or attaching sentiments.

You Accept Yourself the Way You Were Created
You are able to accept yourself and your flaws without thinking there is anything wrong with you on the inside. Love is an inside job, but is often mistaken for an external job. It does not look at just the beauty but sees the soul and the character, and embraces all, including the flaws of the other party, without being judgmental. As you embrace your flaws, you learn to work on them, knowing that they only lead and teach you about any growth needed.

Your Partner Truly Loves Him/Herself
If your partner has also experienced self-love, he/she is able to express love freely without you having to ask if he/she loves you. Love is an action. Love not revealed and

expressed naturally is forced love. When someone loves you, his/her actions and demeanor shows it all and you will not need to ask a thing! Your partner, as a sign of the love you both have and share, must show affection coupled with love.

If you have to ask your partner how much he or she loves you, you are in for a transaction. You are bartering for something in return for what you are giving. You must either give it willingly, expecting nothing in return, or do not give it at all. The reason we believe we must always be paid back is that we set unrealistic expectations based on the "conditioning" we taught ourselves or were taught from childhood. You must however, discard all of these notions to experience love first. The love you have is the love you give. The love you do not have will only get you hurt or broken when you start to ask for it. Love will never change, no matter whom you are with. It is a constant and it is indeed a beautiful thing. Never stop loving while living. When you stop loving, you stop living!

 NUGGET 10

Embracing Your Singleness

Being single is a state for the fragile heart. You may feel lonely at times and want to be in someone's arms, but you do not want to get hurt again, even though you may have to be vulnerable. The fragility of your heart is key to protecting yourself from falling for mere words that are not backed up with actions. It is sometimes difficult for men to decipher a woman who is playing them or using them to buy time. This is because it may appear that she is playing hard to get.

The reality is that if she is the one, she will be willing to loosen up when you step aside and stop calling her for a couple of days. On the other hand, a woman should also learn not to be too quick to let her emotions jump in and make her think it is love when it may just be infatuation.

Connect with Your Spirituality Daily

Singleness sets the time and space for you to connect to your spirituality daily through meditation and prayer. It is a time to have a solid relationship with God, and this will set the foundation for everything you do in life. The more you connect with the Spirit of God within you, the more you are able to purge all your negative thoughts.

You learn to discern right from wrong, and know when to take a step back and when to move forward. Daily affirmations and silent prayers can help guide your steps as you work and walk each day. Spirituality is not about religion, but about building, a solid foundation in a relationship with God and allowing Him guide and guard you throughout life's journey.

Identify Your Needs

The single phase of life is a good place to identify your needs. You may still have wants in terms of physical appearance, but this should be at the bottom of your list. You should prioritize your needs and standards in the correct order.

Create a checklist so that when you meet someone, you are able to check off many the items on your list, if not everything. Do not drop your standards to please a man. You should also not be too demanding.

Do not set any unrealistic expectations that cannot be met by anyone. Always remember that a man will keep pushing until he gets you to give in, but your needs may not be in line with his demands. Buying the eighty-dollar lingerie to please him and get him in the mood is not equivalent to him meeting your needs; instead, it's satisfying momentary pleasure while he may not have you in the picture for long-term purposes.

Let your needs lead you to think about what you are being offered, and learn to walk away if your needs are not aligned to the demands. Men, on the other hand, need to slow down and stop showering a woman with gifts from the very beginning. It is good for both men and women to identify their needs ahead of the game. Always refer to your needs mentally when on a date.

THE LONELY MOMENTS

Being lonely while single signifies a time to connect with yourself and discover something new about yourself. There is always still something to be revealed. We never stop learning about ourselves, until we die. Life is all about learning. Learning allows us to grow. Growing, in turn, makes us become more mature, and the more mature we are, the less trouble we will get into when trying to look for love in the wrong places.

> *Being lonely means it is time to connect with God and grow up spiritually. In solitude and stillness lie clarity. In moments when you feel lonely, take time to connect with your inner being in stillness and hear God speak to your heart.*

Build a firm foundation in and with God and see how He will order your steps in the right direction. What worked for me when I was going through singleness was to be still. I started gardening, where I could hear God speak to me through the plants and nature. God normally speaks to us through everything in life, but we sometimes do not connect because we are often engulfed in the things of life than we are in our spirituality.

The lonely moments are also good for soul-searching. Trace your steps back to every area of your life, things you ignored or never paid attention to. Scan through the lessons learned from the past. Loneliness signifies something is missing and by soul-searching, you can really place your finger on that very thing that seems to leave a void in you.

This is also a good time to spend time with yourself. Do the things you enjoy, and travel. Visit the spa, pick up a new hobby, create a bucket list of things you have not done before and start doing those things. Explore, become adventurous, and find ways to keep yourself busy while loving yourself daily and walking closer to God for directions and guidance.

What Women Need to Understand

You may have met a man who happens to have potential, but you have to remember that certain things you do, whether consciously or unconsciously, may drive the man away. Little things we sometime ignore actually do mean something to someone else. Here are some things to consider:

You have unrealistic expectations
You have created a laundry list of what you are looking for in a man and it all looks like something from the movies. You may be dreaming of having an Idris Elba or Eric Benet, but you have to realize men are different and outward looks can be very deceptive. If you do not get to know the man behind the looks, you may never really realize his full potential, which means you, are going to miss out on opportunities to discover the man you just met.

Dating should be fun and exploratory. It is not a one-time date and you suddenly know who the man is on the same day. It is a gradual process of discovery.

Give up those unrealistic expectations, quit waiting for him to open the door always, learn to relax, and have fun. Think about it as if you are going on a shopping spree and trying on different dresses before knowing what actually fits.

You are too demanding
You expect someone who will be committed before getting to know the real you. You constantly talk about commitment and not wanting a time-waster. This actually makes you sound and look desperate. You need to relax and allow things to flow naturally. You should date for at least three to four months before you start thinking of anything. Remember, you do not know him well and you do not want to rush things that you will later regret.

You expect him to provide you with your wants right from the very start. Do not keep talking about your wants. Dating is about two people learning if the relationship is worth taking to the next level while getting to know each other. Slow down your thought process and demands. You may need to work on your personal issues first before looking for someone who will solve them for you.

> *Do not see dating as the ultimate lead to marriage. You have to learn about your partner, know and understand them first.*

You also have to be willing to contribute to your relationship while dating. This helps set the pace and gain a good understanding of what you are willing to bring to the table.

The phone calls are driving him insane
He has not called you for a while and you have decided to chase him around with your phone calls. You want to know where he is at all times and why he has not called you. You have to learn to give a man his space. When you learn to respect his space, you will enjoy the time you spend together. You have to remember that you are not the only person in his life. He may be testing you by not calling all the time, or it may be that he is busy or giving you space for your "me" time. Always wait for an explanation before jumping to conclusions about why he has not called.

I know you may say there are male players, but you can easily tell if a man is playing or not. If you try to call once and he sends you a message that he will call back, learn to wait for his return call before picking up your phone to dial again.

You are too clingy

You want to be around him all the time and want everyone to know that you are dating. You have to learn to be independent. Some men do not like clingy women. You have to learn to be your own person, and do not expect him to treat you like his daughter. You should act like the grown woman that you are. Stop trying to play the role of his mother as well. You are still a girlfriend and it is still dating. He has the choice to walk away and find someone else that will meet his standards.

> *Every man and woman needs space to be alone. If you choke a man, you leave him with no other option than to walk away from the relationship.*

Calling him all the time, sending text messages, or wanting to spend all your time with him alone will only push him further away from you. Do not get me wrong – there is a time to be with him and a time to be alone. There is time for everything under the sun (Ecclesiastes 3). Try to understand him and do not push or force the relationship. Let everything fall into place, and pray. If he is meant to complement you, he will, and if he is not, nothing can change that. Do not make him tag you as crazy or possessive. This may be a sign of your insecurities or painful past. Make sure you are independent. Men like independent women who do not dominate their space or try to manipulate them. Remember, love is not manipulative and does not seek after self.

All your friends know your business
Your friends have all the information about the two of you. You cannot seem to stop talking about what your friends think about your relationship. Your friends are not you, and you need to be able to take responsibility for your decisions. Keep your relationship between the two of you. No one needs to know what is going on between you. Adding third parties to your business only destroys what you have. A relationship should be between two people and not more.

Once you know you are ready to date, stop doing all of the above and learn to be you. You do not have to pretend or become too demanding. Do not be overly suspicious of his movements or business. Do not act desperate, either. Learn to take a day at a time and let things run smoothly. This is the only way you will find out if the relationship will go further or not. Doing this will get you into the arms of the right man, while doing the aforementioned things will drive the man further away from you.

You Need to Realize You Hold the Keys
Some of us women need to realize that we hold the keys to paradise. Not everyone enters into the kingdom of heaven. Heaven is a place selected for some, not all. As a woman, your assets are your paradise. You need to learn to value why God made you so endowed with these. You cannot keep giving the keys to paradise to every man you meet and get hurt in the process. Paradise is not a cheap place or a common marketplace. It should be reserved for the one who deserves to be with you and deserves to have you.

Letting everyone in will only create grounds for soul ties, as I explained in Nugget #3. Do not leave your soul tied to other people when the relationship will only end after the man has crossed through River Jordan. A man who really wants to be with you will not require that you give up anything. He may try, but it is your decision that will determine if he can actually get you to give the keys up. Giving up your keys is your own decision and doing, not his, so you will have to own that moment and realize it serves as a lesson for you to learn something for the future.

One of the reasons most women give in to sex is because they think it will be hard to find someone who would not ask for it, or they have been alone for a long while without a date. Giving up your sugar for a cheap brand of tea is not ideal and it can seem like you are running a charitable organization with your God-given gifts that are meant to be cherished.

> *Never allow the fear of being alone to drive you into someone's arms or to give up your keys to paradise, for five to twenty minutes' pleasure.*

Choosing to send your nude pictures to another or posting half-nude pictures on social media is a sign that you do not know how valuable and worthy you are. Lonely moments are supposed to be a time of reflection and connection with God to gain knowledge and strength. This is the love you need while single, before the man finds you.

The first step is to know who you are, and once you know who you are, you realize that giving yourself up easily is to your own disadvantage. The key is to love yourself enough to value your keys as an asset given to you by God.

You Choose to Focus on Outward Appearance
No one wants to date anyone who is not good-looking. Good looks sometimes matter, but you must look beyond the outward and deep into the inward to find and connect to the character of the man. Looks may fool you. As you know, the devil also comes disguised as an angel of light, but he has no light within. He may look good but he may abuse, use or manipulate you. Love will not do any of those to you. Love does not hurt.

It is essential that you learn to know the man behind the mask. Be friends with him. Friends tend to open up more to each other than two people in a relationship. Being friends will reveal the sides of him you may never have seen if you kicked the relationship off with dating. He may try to impress you or plan a strategy that you know nothing about. It is best to learn a lot more about him, his background, family, work and more as his friend. Learn what his needs are and see how they match up with yours. Figure out how you both connect spiritually and emotionally.

Always remember that looks change with age and what looks good to the eyes now may not be appealing later on in life.

You do not want to base your relationship on looks but on how you both can connect, love each other, be there for each other through thick and thin, and support each other's purpose throughout life.

You Sometimes Have to Massage His Ego
You sometimes have to massage a man's ego. Men are wired differently from women. We women run on emotions more than men do. Men use their ego to hide their emotions. He is human and emotional. You have to know and understand him. Know how to communicate with him. Do not make him feel uncomfortable or like you've stepped on his ego. Love him for who he is and not what you want him to be. Cut him some slack sometimes and let him be himself.

What Men Need to Understand

Meeting a woman of your dreams is not that hard, but what makes it harder is the way you sometimes approach women. As documented in my book *Love, Sex, Lies and Reality*, the first thing on a man's mind is sex, and sex cannot really determine which relationship works best for you. Below are some things worth noting:

The Act of Having Sex Is a Thought
Sex comes to mind based on your thinking or thought process. Whatever you feed your thoughts determines what you are made of and your outcome in that moment. If all you think about is sex, all you will aim to achieve is having sex. If you think about abstinence, you will aim at remaining celibate.

Always remember that your body is first the temple of God. You were created in His image and after His Likeness.

Sleeping with every woman you meet may lead to your acquiring diseases of unknown and known origins. You may say the condom exists, but you have to realize it can rip off at any time and you can still acquire some sexually transmitted diseases (STDs) with the condom. Envision her as your sister and always think about what you will not have anyone do to her.

You need to learn to put your rods down. Moses knew when to use his rod and when to put it down. You do not have to part every Red Sea you come across. Doing so will only leave room for your soul to be tied to too many women. You can end up become involved in a relationship that can shape or break your life.

She May Look Delectable But May Be Dangerous

You may like what you see, but you have to remember that what you see is not always what you get. The packaging may be very appealing, but the content could be explosive. Always remember that people sometimes pretend to be what they are not. A woman may look like what you really think you need, but may not necessarily be "the one" you need. Looks can be deceptive.

Getting to know her well is vital. First, on a friendship platform, after which you can determine if you want to move forward. Friends reveal more to each other than when dating.

The biblical story of Samson should come to mind. He was a very strong man but gave in to the looks and locks of Delilah, a woman whom he was not supposed to be with due to her background (Judges 16). She seduced him and persuaded him to give up the secret to his strength. She was paid by the rulers to find out what Samson's secret was. She eventually found out after several attempts and revealed her findings to the rulers of Philistine.

You may wonder what this has to do with you. Well, looks can be deceiving and she may be another trap to your downfall. Sex may be great, but it may not be what you need. You may only end up settling to be in a mess. Remember, Samson had no clue what he was getting into either. Samson settled for his own will and forgot about God's will for his life.

It is essential that you think and connect to God's will and plan for you, rather than follow your own will and face a situation that will leave you devastated, thanks to the lies you told yourself and the truth you avoided.

Is She Who You Want, or Is She the Woman You Need?
God's promise is to supply all your needs according to His riches in glory (Philippians 4:19). However, you seem to focus on your wants due to not connecting with God or seeking His counsel but going with your own decisions. It may be you have just gone through a breakup and you do not want to take the time to heal. You meet someone whose looks got your attention (a distraction) who seems to tell you what you want to hear and you think will help you cope with your current situation. All you need to do is

pray, but you ignore that step and follow your own logical thinking. You may think God's answer for you is not what you need to hear, but what you have sketched out as your own master plan must be executed with no time wasted.

Always remember that not everything that looks good to the eyes will taste good when eaten. The presentation layers may be appealing, but the contents may not be of benefit to you. Learn to focus on your needs and find a woman who shares the same as you in terms of needs, values, visions/dreams – someone compatible and complementary. You both can meet each other at the same place and build a life of love together. Trust God's timing, not yours.

> *We often look for the quickest and shortest route to get things done, but learning to be patient and waiting for the right and divine timing of God saves us from getting in a mess.*

Always remember, "The blessing of the Lord makes rich and He adds no sorrow to it" (Proverbs 10:22). That is why when you learn to wait, you will find a wife and know it is indeed a good thing you have found.

Do Not Compare Her to Your Mom or Any Other Woman

There are men who look for qualities of their mothers in a girlfriend. You always have to remember, if you are such a man, that your mother is different from your girlfriend. No two people are the same or act the same. You can never marry your mother and should not be comparing her with anyone else. Individuals are designed/created by God to be unique in their ways.

Do not compare your girlfriend to anyone you have dated in the past. Everyone is different and you have to be able to accept her for who she is. Comparison is a relationship-killer. Do not ruin your relationship by doing this. Learn to accept her with her flaws and love her for who she is.

Do Not Control Her...Learn to Respect Her
You may always want to be in control, but you have to remember that love has nothing to do with control. Ego is what drives control. Ego is an illusion. The reason why you want to be controlling is that you do not want her to think you are weak, but you have to remember we all have flaws. A woman who truly loves you does not need you to control her, but will accept you the way you are irrespective of your weaknesses, without judging you. The more you show her respect, listen to her and love her, the better your relationship becomes and the more you grow into each other while learning about each other.

The respect you show her will be reciprocated when you learn to treat her as your friend, best friend and girlfriend. You may say she is supposed to submit to you but you always have to learn to submit to her. You may disagree on some issues, but the way you handle it will determine how she responds. You do not have to sound controlling or raise your voice. Conduct yourself in a way where you communicate effectively with a soft tone, not sounding too macho. It is not a sign of weakness, as you may think, but one of strength. The more you learn to value her contributions to your relationship, the more she will respect and value you. If you find your conversations getting heated, let her know you need to go for a walk. Think things through while on your walk, calm down, regroup, and go back to resolve issues. Do not let anything go over a day before resolving conflicts.

What Both Men and Women Need to Understand

Whatever happened in the past should stay in the past. Learn to make every day a brand new day, just as God designed it to be. If God does not remember our past sins when we ask Him for forgiveness, why do we keep reopening the can of worms? You cannot change what happened in the past but you can utilize the lessons learned in the present and future. Do not think of every person you meet as someone who will hurt you.

If you have truly healed and forgiven yourself and others, this should not have to come to light again. Generalizing and stereotyping are blessing-blockers that you must let go of. Always see others through the eyes of God and do not try to play judge. Learn to be the "authentic" you at all times. You do not need to impress anyone. If he or she is meant to be with you, it will happen without you trying to force or push it to happen.

Do not place material value on your relationship. Materialism will only destroy what you have. Talk about everything with each other. Discuss whatever bothers you without holding back. Communication is one of the keys to a long-lasting relationship. Learn to communicate in a manner that does not appear rude or offensive.

Everyone comes with flaws, and no one is perfect. You have to learn to accept your partner and their flaws. Note I said flaws, not baggage. No one should bring baggage from the past into the present relationship. Doing so will only show that you still need to revert to yourself, heal, forgive and find who God truly made you to be. Do not use your partner's flaws as a source to talk down on him or her.

Finances can put a hole in your relationship. It is important to talk about finances early in your relationship. Many relationships end due to financial arguments. Divide responsibilities and document schedules if needed. Lay it all out on the table so that when the time comes, this will not become an issue.

Be honest and open about everything. Keeping secrets can ruin a great relationship. Always be open and honest, and ask questions when you are unsure. Communicate, communicate, and communicate! It does not hurt when you do, but it does when you do not. Honesty and openness about issues can get them resolved faster than not opening up, or being dishonest or shady. If there is anything you are not comfortable with, do not pretend you are but instead be open and honest. Remember, we are all on land to learn.

Your relationship is not a competition. You are not better than your partner, especially when you are a couple and have moved past friendship. Relationships are about helping each other grow and walk in purpose. Do not see yourselves as competitors, especially for those who are homeowners. Do not try to outdo each other but always be supportive of each other's goals, visions and purpose.

Trying to compete shows that you are not ready to be a couple or that you have not yet identified your true self and still need to find who you really are.

Walk in purpose. Finding someone to date or be with is easier than being patient and finding someone who shares your values, your purposes are aligned, they are compatible and they complement you. However, when you learn to wait and you have found yourself, loved yourself and embraced your flaws, it becomes easier to find that person who you can be friends with, become best friends, lovers and eventually husband and wife. The more your purpose aligns with that of your partner, the easier it will be to walk in unity. (I am not saying there will not be conflicts, but there will be an easy way out of handling situations when you know, understand each other and are in harmony.)

 NUGGET 11

Walking in Your Purpose

We sometimes need to fall in order to rise and find ourselves so we can fully know who we are and find our purpose in life. As you begin the journey to a new you and to walking in your purpose, you will meet four groups of people.

Purpose Helpers

Your purpose helpers are those people who will come into your life to help you move towards fulfilling your purpose. They are not necessarily people you may know, but God planted them in your path to assist you with the tasks you have lined up with your purpose. God opens doors through your purpose helpers to help you get into the right places at the right time and meet the right people you need to know to accomplish purpose tasks.

Your purpose helpers will encourage you and help you move to the next level. They stimulate your growth towards purpose.

Purpose Pushers

Your purpose pushers are those who get under your skin to push you forward. They are always asking when the next move is. They make you become a go-getter if you are not already one. They do not relent, pushing you beyond your comfort zone so that you can step into places you once viewed as uncomfortable or undoable.

Purpose Stoppers

We come across certain people who are not excited or happy about us progressing. We call these purpose stoppers. Some of them tend to block your prospects. They want to know about your ideas but are not willing to help you get to the right resources, the ones will help bring your ideas to life. They may ask you to keep coming back to visit them at their offices or to meet up, but they have plans to steal your ideas rather than help you.

Purpose Killers

Purpose killers never wish you well; instead, they look for opportunities to make you fail. Joseph in the Bible had purpose killers. Potiphar's wife was one of Joseph's purpose killers. She tried to seduce him to redirect his attention away from what God had called him to do. Purpose killers try to put the flame out on directions you can take to flourish.

We were all created and are here on earth for a purpose. The phases and stages we go through in life, the people we meet both good and bad, are all part of what leads us towards finding, fulfilling and living our individual purpose.

> *We often do not get close to finding what our purpose is, until we have become broken beyond our expectations.*

Something major usually happens that pushes us in the direction of purpose. It sometimes feels like the point of giving up on oneself. You may feel frustrated; you may have tried everything in your power and have become exhausted of ideas or cannot seem to find a solution to the problem. At that point, the only choice is to connect with your spirituality, and there you find yourself questioning why God brought you here and made you go through all that pain.

The reality is, most of the time you were not connecting to God but to your thoughts and making your own decisions. It was you living out your "prodigal" journey – the phase where you let God have a part of you while you held on to the rest, which looked like the best course of action to you at that point in time. The most difficult part of life is giving up what we enjoy doing the most or the part of us that we told God not to take care of. We thought we could handle it all alone, but have now failed at doing so. Hence, we have no choice but to go back to Him and give it all up.

People will sometimes push you out of their lives towards your purpose. Do not dwell so much on the distractions that show up in form of hurt or pain, but instead thank them for pushing you towards your destiny. The relationship that did not work out had a season, a reason and a purpose. All you need to do is take the lessons learned from it and move on in newness. Always remember that every relationship serves a purpose for a season and a reason.

You may wonder why I shared on purpose. Once you recognize and connect with your purpose, your vision becomes clearer. You also gain clarity into the kind of partner you need going forward. Recognizing your purpose allows you to select a partner whose purpose aligns with yours. Purpose is the reason why we were created, and without working and walking in purpose, we will be held back to our old ways. You become each other's purpose helper while building strongly into one another and praying together.

 NUGGET 12

Building into Your Relationship

The moment you start dating again, you will have to consider the lessons you learned through your journey. Those lessons, along with this nugget, should help you stay focused and on track without having to bend or break to please anyone. The only person you need to please is God.

Watch the actions of your date carefully and ensure they match up with their words. Do not be gullible or try to rush anything. A worthwhile relationship will not require that you rush or overdo yourself. Here are some of the things you need to put into consideration:

You Can Both Survive Without Sex While Dating

You should not be having sex outside marriage (technically speaking). Men try hard to stay away from this topic (and some women do too). Sex can cloud your judgment and may lead you into the arms of someone who will eventually hurt you. It is more important that you get to know and understand each other. Sex can hide a lot about the other person and the issues will linger on until the scales fall off your eyes.

> *Being caught up in a sexual relationship clogs up your ability to focus on other areas of your relationship.*

You will also save yourself from worrying about unexpected pregnancy, diseases or condoms ripping off and causing medical havoc.

Do not get distracted from what is needed in a relationship by spending so much time on the physical. You may have to pay a huge price for it later on. It is better to avoid distractions that can derail you from where you need to be.

I know you may say you need to test-drive the car before driving off the sales parking lot, but you cannot completely know what is under the hood even if you test-drive the car. There may be some lurking issues, which are not visible to the eyes and may later come to haunt you. I touched on solutions of getting your partner into the bedroom act in my book *Love, Sex, Lies and Reality*. You can read more on how to help your partner when it comes to sex when married in the book.

Spiritual Compatibility Is More Important than Physical Attraction

"As iron sharpens iron, so one person sharpens another." – Proverbs 27:17

Make sure you are spiritually compatible. You have to be able to sharpen each other spiritually and stand in the gap prayerfully. Dating someone who is unequally yoked with you spiritually will only result in conflict. You will not be able to pull stronger together. One of you will appear more overzealous than the other. Deep has to be able to call to deep, and you have to be able to speak life and the word of God into each other's lives.

Sowing the spiritual seeds into each other's lives while dating and courting lays a foundation for your marriage. Be with someone who can pray for and with you, and you can both encourage and lift each other up spiritually. This should be at the top of your list when trying to find a partner. The more you are spiritually connected, the fewer conflicts you will face in your relationship.

> *Be mindful of those who pretend to be spiritual just to get into a relationship. Remember to put every spirit to the test to ensure it is in line with the will of God for your life.*

If you are both spiritually connected, your purpose will be aligned and you can easily discern this. Spirituality is not about attending a church service or night vigil, but about your personal relationship with God. Your connection with God through the Holy Spirit will reveal a lot about your partner's spirituality as well.

How You Resolve Issues Can Help You Both Grow

Being able to hold conversations without raising your voices but instead amicably resolving whatever issues you have in your relationship will help both of you grow as individuals first and then as a couple. You need to realize that a relationship is about two people who are willing to commit to each other selflessly despite their individual differences. You have to be willing to listen to each other without talking over one another. The more you learn to sit down and discuss rather than argue, the more mature your relationship becomes.

Do not try to prove you know it all when having a discussion. No one knows it all but God. Some men find it hard to listen to women. They believe they cannot possibly have any good suggestions to bring to the table. This is, however, a big mistake. Relationships exist because two people agree to work, unite and commit to each other. Active listening is part of the commitment made. Do not talk down on each other but instead learn to listen to the details and come to a place of agreement together.

The more you can resolve issues, the stronger you will build into one another and it will make your relationship stronger.

Finding Common Grounds

Finding common grounds while dating helps you set the pace for activities you can do together when not working. It may be outdoors or indoors, but ensure you both share similar interests that can help keep the flame of your relationship burning stronger. This allows you to connect in ways that can improve not only your activities together but also your communication skills.

If he enjoys watching soccer and you do too, it makes it more fun when you both chime in during a game. You can also cook and participate in household chores together. Have a picnic in the yard or the park. Do things that bring in color and excitement to your relationship while dating. You will find this becomes part of your daily living. Finding common grounds not only brightens your relationship but brings you closer together more often. Affection is needed to keep a relationship going, and this is one of the ways you can show each other affection.

NUGGET 13

Bottom Line/Conclusion

Do you have a game plan, or are you just going with the flow? Do you look back and trace your steps to where you started from – your childhood, friends or experiences – to see if this may have resulted in the choices you make when it comes to dating? Do you need to step up your game plan? Do you really know who you are? Do you understand your needs? Do you know your purpose?

Ask yourself these questions as you embark on your journey of being single with a fragile heart.

Singleness is a phase everyone must face in life, but understanding this fragile state requires connection with God and oneself, and embracing this stage as part of one's growth in life.

You have to find yourself right from your teenage years, which is where all the experiment begins, and so does the prodigal son's journey. You must learn to love yourself before loving someone else. You must first learn to be happy for you. No one else can give you the happiness you have not yet given to yourself.

Finding Happiness Within

The empty void in the life of a single man or woman sometimes drives them to think that happiness can be found with someone else. The reality is that happiness starts and ends with you. No one can make you happy except you, connecting with your inner being and deriving happiness through love.

Being single is a stage in our lives where we live with the fragility of our hearts, and it all boils down to exploring, discovering, connecting and finding ourselves. We also learn about us, get hurt, and grow, becoming stronger and wiser. All these lead to us finding the purposes for which God created us.

Finding ourselves and connecting back to God leads to the healing and forgiveness process (which is ongoing for the rest of our lives). We can only align our lives with His Will when we let go of everything…giving it all back to God and shifting from our comfort zone to evolve into the new ways laid down by God for us according to His Purpose for which He created us. Love transforms our lives daily when we come closer to Him, and in return, we bring love into our lives through a deeper relationship with God as we surrender to His Will and we let go of our ego.

> *Excuses are signs of insecurity and incompetence. You have to realize that your habits and choices will determine what happens on your journey.*

All the lessons are about you waking up to reality and learning that you still have so much to learn and grow into or with. The key is to find your purpose through all the experiences you have gone through, knowing that your tests and experiences lead to your testimonies and ministry in life. This in turn leads you to your purpose. The scars you may have acquired along the way are not meant to hold you back but to help others going through similar situations heal. That is all part of the love you connect with and to when you find who you really are created to be.

The most difficult moments of our lives often lead to the brightest and best parts we live. It is not always about the pain, at the end of the day, but about how the lessons transformed and shaped us. Despite all the heartaches and heartbreaks we face, we end up discovering who we truly are and this leads to a change. We are no longer defined by the past but we have emerged to become a person of purpose, knowing the real reason why we are created and what we need to accomplish before we depart the earth. It is indeed a new dawn, a new beginning and a new you. It sure feels good to be free of all that pain. Now you are alive again!

Learn to Love Yourself More Daily

There is so much love you can give to yourself when you learn to be patient, kind, and not easily angered. You learn to trust yourself while speaking the truth in all honesty with and to yourself. Do not keep a record of wrongs or chase after evil desires of revenge. When you truly love yourself, there is nothing to boast about or seek validation for because you know you were made complete. You become selfless in the process. It also becomes easier for you to embrace lessons learned along your journey, knowing they serve as a growth outlet.

Always remember this:
What cannot shape you will not break you.
What cannot mend you will not mold you.
What cannot plant you, will not grow you.
Those who cannot love you will leave you.
However, you must continue to love yourself. Love starts with self-love.

Learn to embrace who you are without allowing anyone to alter you. Be authentic and let the world see that you are real. Many may not embrace you, but what matters most is that you know who you are and you are living the "you" God created. Being free-spirited and connecting to the Spirit of God in you allows you to live in God's will for you.

Do Not Try to Change for Anyone

Remain authentic. Be true to yourself. Let kindness, integrity and grace lead you. Be a blessing to others always, not a burden. Place people before things and value your relationships with one another. Be at peace with everyone.

Do not try to change yourself for anyone or try changing someone to who you want him or her to be. You were created as you for a reason and a purpose, and only you can live it to the fullest. Trying to change for someone will only result in you getting hurt and becoming unhappy.

Control Your Emotions

Your emotions can lead you in the wrong direction when you do not pay attention to detail or to words uttered. It can be easy to think you are in love, but it may just be infatuation and lust with no love in the equation. Learning to control your emotions will prevent you from falling for infatuation and lust while instead focusing on love. Learn to think with your head and not your emotions at the very beginning. Becoming emotional about a relationship will lead to making assumptions and creating scenarios that do not exist.

Do not be too quick to make assumptions but instead, communicate effectively with others while being polite, compassionate and patient. Sometimes you may allow your emotions to make you become fretful when you focus on what others will think or say about you. You should never allow the fear of what others think or could think hold you back from healing. Your journey is about you and no one else. Only you can make the decisions that can shape, break or mold you. It is your life. Own every moment and make it count. Owning your moments and putting your emotions under lock will help you think of ways to overcome instead of ways to hold back.

You may also be going through some rough times and when you run on emotions alone, you take out your pain on others. You have to be willing to learn from everyone you meet, knowing that each person serves a purpose in your journey. Whether it is a painful or painless experience, some will teach, some will shape, some will bend or break you while others will change you. Overall, you are learning and growing. With growth comes the knowledge and wisdom you need to become a better, stronger and wiser you. Always remember this:

> *The storm you face is your teacher. The experience you gain is your lesson. The life you make out of it is your blessing.*
>
> *Always remember, the teacher teaches a lesson that becomes a blessing. Embrace the storm and watch your life change as you utilize the lessons. Your better days lie ahead...just hold on!*

The more you realize every experience results in a lesson, the more you will control your emotions and the quicker you will heal and turn your lessons into blessings. Remember, life is short and no one is perfect. Live, laugh, learn and love most of all. Life is indeed a gift. Live right while you still have the chance.

> *At the end of the day, what matters most is not what tore you apart but the love that binds and heals your heart.*

Learn to Love Yourself First

You cannot give love when you have not experienced love. You cannot give love you have not received. You have to learn to love yourself first. This can be achieved by connecting to the One who is love and first gave us love through birth. The more you walk with God and trust Him completely for everything and in everything, the more you connect with Him spiritually and let Him guide you all the way. Love is what we are born with; love is what makes us complete when we fully come to the awareness of the real us. Embracing yourself, your flaws, and your confidence will help you realize that this fragile state of singleness creates the awareness for you to trust yourself, protect yourself, be kind, be patient with yourself and learn to speak the truth to yourself always.

Something to Remember: Without living, there will be no learning. Without learning, there will be no growth. Without growth, there will be no change. The only way you learn is by trying. You may make mistakes, but you have to remember that doing so will lead to change. Be willing to learn from experiences, grow, and live to become better, not bitter.

Always remember that people come into your lives for a reason, a season and a purpose. Others are for a lifetime. All come into our lives to teach, break, shape, mend, bend and help us grow. Do not hold on to what is supposed to last for a season, thinking it is for a lifetime. Prayerfully ask God to show you who belongs in a particular season and for what reason.

I leave you with this: Love is bigger than life. Love has no limits. Love does not separate color, race or background. Love is ONE and you are one with love. It is important to connect with love before connecting with someone else. The love you have is the love you can share. You have to love yourself first by finding the real you. Once you do, connect with love and let God love on you. Love is what we are all born with and it is part of our lives. Let love live and abide in you as you find and love yourself. Only then can you find another to share the love with. Only then, can you truly walk and work in your purpose.

Q&A

1. How do I know who I am at the exploration stage?

The key is to start connecting to your soul and spirit (the Spirit of God) within you. The more you find who you are in God at an early stage in life, the less you will enter situations that can make you walk down the wrong path.

Many times when we do not know who we are, we go with the regular flow and think that what is normal is right. The exploration phase is designed to help you connect with the Spirit of God, find who you are and start to explore life as God designed it, but the disconnection from God and connection to the world often makes people think that rejection from others is a sign of failure. No matter what you do in life, others will still judge you. The views of others, however, will not help you make progress but will instead deter you from God's plans and purpose for your life.

2. How do I know who the wrong or right friends are, or if I am in the wrong/right mix?

You will feel that something is not right. Paying attention and listening to the still, small voice will help you connect to the Spirit of God within you. You will definitely hear the Spirit of God tell you not to take that step. There will be conflict with the still voice and the controlling voice that tells you to go ahead and do it anyway, even when you feel that it is not the right thing to do.

The right friends will always be in accord with what your spirit is telling you to do or abide by. They will also respect your decisions and encourage you to believe in those decisions. They will support and respect your choices. Always remember, whatever decisions you make affect you and come with consequences, positive or negative.

3. How do I untie my soul from my ex?

Untying your soul requires you to forgive yourself for what has happened that may have resulted in you trying to hold on to the memories. Forgive your ex; knowing that you cannot change the past but you can make the future better. You also want to leave room for friendship. This is because the world is a small place and you never know if you will need their help in the future. Let your ex know you have forgiven him/her. Occupy your time and mind with activities that will prevent you from thinking about any situation that may dampen your spirit or make you feel down. What is gone is gone, but you can always learn from the lessons from the past.

4. Why do breakups hurt so much?

Breakups hurt because you set too high of expectations and those were not met. Setting too high of expectations can often result in disappointments and loss of confidence. It is always good to begin a relationship with an open mind and friendship. Gradually becoming friends will let you know if the relationship will work out or not. It is okay to have standards and to align your standards and needs with those of your partner.

Learn to take a day of friendship at a time so that you do not feel let down or heartbroken. Do not set unrealistic expectations and know that your partner is an individual who cannot read your mind but also has standards to be met. Do not dwell so much on the pain (which is all in your thoughts) or the emotions, but instead focus on the lessons from the breakup. Let those teach you and be a blessing, as well as a reminder that greater things lie ahead of you when you learn to be patient.

5. I love my partner but he/she is narcissistic. How can I help him/her change?

The truth is that you cannot change anyone. The narcissist has many issues that are not dealt with or addressed. Your partner will have to address these issues alone or with the help of a specialist. You may try to talk things out and see if it will work, but you alone know what you are experiencing or have experienced. Do what is best for you and keeps you safe. Remember, you only have one life to live and you alone will give account for it.

6. I think my partner is a player. What do I do?

You should sit down and talk things over. Always remember your needs, visions and purpose. Ensure they align with those of your partner. If your partner is not ready for commitment but you are, it may be a good time to sit down and discuss this. The question is, can you really love someone who does not respect or value you? He/she must know your worth and treat you the way you deserve to be treated.

7. Why should I forgive someone who really hurt me?

Forgiveness is not for the one who hurt you. Forgiveness is for you. You should forgive so that you can let go of the hurt. Learn to discard the emotions that still tie you to them and find peace within yourself. As I stated in the nugget, telling someone that you forgive them is not a sign of weakness but of strength and courage to move you towards where you need to be. You not only find peace, you are also free from being bound to them by the hurt or pain you carry.

8. How can I start the soul-searching process?

You can start by going down memory lane to the very beginning: your very first date. Sometimes you may have to go deep into family values to soul-search if there were patterns you observed in the family that you also practiced. You can also journal your thoughts down memory lane to help you identify the repeated patterns.

About the Author

Kemi Sogunle is an **author, writer, speaker and professional life and relationship coach.** She is the **Founder/CEO** of the **nonprofit** organization (501c3), Love Not Hurt, an organization that promotes self-development, building healthier and stronger relationships while living with purpose. She is also the host of a talk show named after her first book, "Love, Sex, Lies and Reality."

She is **dedicated** to helping others **transform** their lives through self-development and growth, **gaining knowledge** and **understanding of self-love** before becoming involved in a relationship, find what works best and how to stay true to oneself while connecting with others to build solid relationships that will make their lives better not bitter.

She writes and speaks from a personal place and **experience on relationships, healing, forgiveness and purposeful**

living by moving from pain to purpose. Kemi began her journey to becoming a life and relationship coach after her separation and divorce, which led her to soul-searching. She connected to her spirituality while viewing life from a different perspective. She found herself in the process and gained a deep understanding of life and relationships as well as her purpose in life. She shares deep and inspirational messages through her writing and has touched many lives across the globe. She also teaches, motivates and inspires others to become the best version of the person God created them to be on daily basis. She believes that **living truthfully is paramount to long-lasting relationships and healthy living**.

Connect with Kemi

Website: www.kemisogunle.com
Facebook: www.facebook.com/lovesexliesandreality
Twitter: www.twitter.com/kemisogunle
Instagram: www.instagram.com/kemisogunle
Learn about life and relationship coaching with Kemi:
www.kemisogunle.com/life-and-relationship-coaching

www.ingramcontent.com/pod-product-compliance
Lightning Source LLC
Chambersburg PA
CBHW060521090426
42735CB00011B/2318